1 ARMOURED DIVISION IN
OPERATION "POLO"

BY

Major-General J. N. CHAUDHURI,
OBE

The Naval & Military Press Ltd

Published by
The Naval & Military Press Ltd
5 Riverside, Brambleside, Bellbrook
Industrial Estate, Uckfield, East Sussex,
TN22 1QQ England

Tel: +44 (0) 1825 749494

Fax: +44 (0) 1825 765701

www.naval-military-press.com

www.military-genealogy.com

" *My thanks are due to my GSO 1, Lt Col T. K. Mukerji for the help he has given me in reading the proofs, checking the copy, correcting the SD and in fact helping me considerably in the production of this book.*"

JNC

In reprinting in facsimile from the original, any imperfections are inevitably reproduced and the quality may fall short of modern type and cartographic standards.

PREFACE

THIS book has been written mainly to give all those members of 1 Armd Div and the formations and units under command, a composite story, purely from the Divisional point of view, as to the part they played in operation "POLO." A recapitulation of events from the very first stages of the planning, the subsequent stages of training and re-equipping, followed by the actual operations and a summary of lessons learnt, might be useful to refresh their memories of the stages that have to be gone through as well as be of help when further operations are planned. The slight discourse in the opening chapters on political and public reactions is necessary to show how such reactions affect the broader aspects of planning. The book is also designed to fulfil two other purposes. Firstly, to be a historical record for unit and formation libraries and secondly, to be a possible reference book when the whole history of the Indian Army after nationalisation is written.

In the last chapter certain lessons have been dsicussed. To those who feel that these are repetitions of well-known principles, it is interesting to note how these principles re-emphasised themselves in a wholly mobile operation. The object of including them has been to refresh the minds of those who knew them already and bring them to the notice of those who were unaware of them. No claim is made that these lessons are hard and fast rules which must be observed. They are however a sound basis on which planners and commanders can build.

Comparisons are odious and there can be no comparison between the operations in Jammu and Kashmir and the Police Action in Hyderabad. The former was a major war and one into which the Indian Army had gone at short notice. It was fought over difficult terrain, with long vulnerable lines of communication and against a stubborn and well-equipped opposition. The latter was a brief incident, satisfactorily planned and against forces, who after the third day, virtually collapsed. In fact the main thought of the executors of operation "POLO," was to get it over quickly so that at no time would their comrades in Kashmir have to look over their shoulders.

One more thought exists. This book is also intended as a thanksoffering to all ranks of 1 Armd Div and units and formations under command, for their spirit, loyalty, co-operation and behaviour, without which we would not have been so successful. At all stages they upheld the highest traditions of the Indian Army, which, of course, we all knew that they would do.

J. N. CHAUDHURI

Date 6 *July*, 1949.

ARMY HEADQUARTERS,
NEW DELHI.

forward.

This publication on " OPERATION POLO " is an interesting record of the chronological events which led to the solution of the difficult HYDERABAD problem which faced our Government early in 1948. Major-General CHAUDHURI has given his readers, in logical sequence in a very lucid style of writing, a true picture of the events which culminated in the set-up of the present administration of the State. A thoroughly prepared plan and its sound and rapid execution by officers concerned at all levels brought those operations to a very successful end in an incredibly short time.

2. In Chapter XII, the writer has brought out some of the important lessons learnt. These lessons although not new, are yet a reminder of the general principles of warfare which, through lack of experience, perhaps were forgotten or rather overlooked by a number of officers who participated in the execution of the plan.

3. It is a well produced document and is of valuable Military study to all officers, particularly to junior officers.

General,
Commander-in-Chief.
(KM CARIAPPA)

NEW DELHI,
1 Oct 49.

CHAPTER I.

"THE WELDING TOGETHER."

In early February 48 the General Staff at Army HQ were working on Internal Security plans throughout India. In this planning, the question of military intervention in Hyderabad, if so ordered by the Government of India, was naturally considered. Based on this premise, a directive was sent to the then GOCinC, Southern Command, General Sir E. N. Goddard, to prepare a plan for the occupation of Secunderabad by military force, in case it became necessary. As available troops for this operation, Gen Goddard was given the choice of either, HQ 1 Armd Div or HQ 5 Inf Div with certain specified troops under command. Southern Command selected HQ 1 Armd Div and in outline, the force that was allotted to them was

- HQ 1 Armd Div and Div troops
- HQ 1 Armd Bde
    - 17 HORSE
    - 3 CAV
    - 9 DOGRA
- HQ 7 Inf Bde
    - Three infantry battalions
- HQ 9 Inf Bde
    - Three infantry battalions
- HQ Arty 1 Armd Div
    - 1 Fd Regt (SP) (25 prs)
    - 34 (M) A Tk Regt (SP) (of which one bty was non-effective)
    - 9 Para Fd Regt (25 prs)

Three infantry battalions to be specified later.

One troop 18 CAV (the remainder of 18 CAV being under re-organisation and so non-operational).

Southern Command's plan was received at Army HQ during the middle of March 48 and with certain minor amendments, was approved. The operation envisaged a two pronged advance on Hyderabad, the main force moving along the road Sholapur-Hyderabad, a distance of 186 miles and a smaller force moving along the road Bezwada-Hyderabad, a distance of 160 miles. The concentration areas of these two forces were at Sholapur and Bezwada respectively.

Army HQ appreciated that in the event of such a military operation taking place a Civil Administrative Organization might be required to take over administration in the State after the entry of the military force. After much discussion, the nucleus of such an organization was formed about June 1948 and started to train and work in conjunction with HQ, Southern Command. In general, the organization consisted of a Chief Civil Administrator, an IG of Police, and representatives of the Railway, the PWD and the Health Department at the Centre, with a Civil Administrator and DSP for each of the 16 districts of the State. Officers for this set up were found mainly from the Provinces of Bombay, CP and Madras. The planners had realised the need for capturing the capital, Hyderabad City, as soon as possible. As a result, at further discussions it was agreed that the Commander of 1 Armd Div was to have as his main object the rapid seizure of Hyderabad City and so was not to be worried with protection of the Lines of Communication behind his Divisional rear limit. Consequently, Sholapur (Indep) Sub-Area was set up. Their main tasks were, to assist concentration before the operation, hold the border against aggression while concentration was taking place and control administration and protection in rear of the Divisional advance, once operations had started. The whole military operation against Hyderabad was given the code name POLO by Army HQ presumably in memory of the many games of polo that had been played in Secunderabad by so many officers of the Indian Army.

In mid March with the above background the Commander, 1 Armd Div, at that time Maj Gen H. L. Atal, reviewed his resources and examined details of the Division's fitness for POLO. The picture was most discouraging. What little there was concentrated of his Division was stationed in Jhansi. The remainder were widely dispersed. There was an overall shortage of officers and other ranks. The Div HQ had never been exercised with the existing staff, who had in most cases just been posted. There was a forty per cent deficiency of vehicles, personnel, equipment, and tanks. Unit commanders were new to their units, while the units themselves had just been reorganized after partition. This reorganization in some cases, such as 3 CAV was still not complete while 18 CAV could only provide one troop. Of the two infantry brigades allotted to 1 Armd Div for the operation, 7 Inf Bde had just been got together and was training in Poona. The Brigadier and COs were all new. The units were considerably under strength and none of them had worked with tanks before. 9 Inf Bde on the other hand was a fairly well trained brigade. At the time however they were stationed in Ranchi, much too far away to co-ordinate training.

With regard to the supporting arms, the Armd Div Signals were still moving down from JAK force, where they had been rushed at the beginning of the Kashmir operations six months ago. The Armd Div Engineer Group was still employed in Kashmir and so was not available. An " ad hoc " Engineer group, split up over Southern and Western Commands was being assembled to replace them. These engineers were composed of units that had been got together very rapidly and had not worked with armour before, neither were they organized or equipped as assault engineers normally employed with an Armd Div. On the face of it the situation appeared extremely bleak and though the machinery for reinforcements, equipment, etc, was set in motion, stores, equipment, vehicles and personnel came in very slowly. Training was given the highest priority and progress started to be made.

Meanwhile the situation in Hyderabad was obviously fast deteriorating and at the end of April, HQ 1 Armd Div with 1 Armd Bde was given orders to move to Southern Command. Simultaneously with this move, which started at the beginning of May, the Armd Div Commander and Armd Bde Commander were both posted away. A new Divisional Commander, Maj Gen J. N. Chaudhuri was posted taking over on 14 May and Brig. S. D. Verma arrived from the Staff College as Armd Bde Commander, taking over on 4 May. During April also 9 Inf Bde was moved from Ranchi to Bangalore and this brought them not only much nearer but also under HQ, Southern Command.

These large scale moves naturally took up time which could ill be spared from training. The original plan had envisaged certain sub-units of the Armd Bde being lent to other formations for operations. When movement started, one squadron of 17 HORSE was sent to Bezwada to be put under command Madras Area, while one troop of 18 CAV was sent to Jubbulpore to be put under command Jubbulpore (Indep) Sub-Area. The rest of 18 CAV was non-operational.

It will be seen therefore, that by the middle of May, after the first moves had been completed, the Armd Div was still by no means complete. It was widely dispersed between Poona, Dhond, Ahmednagar, Bangalore and Aundh, making control of administration and supervision of training difficult. The Division as a whole had still not worked together, while the two infantry brigades allotted to the Division had never worked with tanks. A new Divisional Commander and Armd Bde Commander had just taken over, the staff and service officers were new and the younger ones untrained, while training was constantly being interrupted by large parties being away from units collecting epuipment.

From the middle of May onwards things started to improve a great deal because units and formations had moved much nearer the Depots. Fresh demands for equipment were placed on Southern Command and with the help of their staff and Col Agya Singh who had been detached specially from Army HQ to assist, equipment started to pour in. The highest credit here must be given to the excellent way in which the IAOC and IEME of Southern Command worked in getting equipment ready. No hours seemed to be too long and the enthusiasm was magnificent. Training was also intensified and with 7 Inf Bde coming under command, combined training between infantry and tanks started to become possible. HQ which had not worked together before started to function as entities and were put through a number of small exercises with Signals to teach them their role. The Armd Div Signals, released from Kashmir joined up. Their experience there had been most useful. The Engineer Group also arrived and started to work with armour as well as to train themselves. This intensified training together with the arrival of new equipment, had an extremely heartening effect on the Division Formations and units started to get to know each other, commanders started to get to know their men and what was most important, the men started to get familiar with their equipment. Morale among the troops which had been dropping before, owing mainly to lack of leave, uncertainty and being away from their families improved very quickly. At last they had got the tools to work with and were learning how to use these tools.

The concentration of the Armd Div, was at this stage, and in fact right up to the last, only a precautionary measure. The Government of India were extremely anxious to settle matters by negotiation, and political talks on the highest level were going on between the two Governments. Various formulæ were evolved but settlement seemed to be as far distant as ever. It is not the intention here to discuss in any detail the various political factors concerned but at this stage the Razakar organization must be mentioned. A militant adjunct of the Ittehad-ul-Musselmin, the political party in power, this organization was expanding rapidly, despite all protests from the Government of India. Numbering over 200,000, armed, aggressive and always ready to take the law into their own hands, the Razakars had permeated to every portion of the State. Reports of their high-handedness, particularly against the Hindus, both in the State and on the borders kept pouring in. Their leader, Kasim Razvi, the power behind the Hyderabad Government, was inciting them with inflammatory speeches. He had said that he and his men would plant the Asaf Jahi flag on the Red Fort in Delhi, that the waters of the Bay of Bengal and the Arabian Sea would lap the feet of the Nizam, and even that Hyderabad would overthrow India.

Despite the negotiations, Hyderabad was re-arming, increasing its armed forces, both civil and military and reorganizing itself militantly. Arms were being obtained by smuggling and the seizure of weapons from non-Muslims legitimately entitled to possess them. The Army was being expanded, so-called refugees from India were being raised into territorial units and " refugee " battalions. The number of armed police were being increased, while even such departments as the Customs and Excise were being issued with a quota of weapons. Hyderabad Radio was carrying on an extensive and bombastic propaganda against the Indian Union. This attitude changed the original appreciation to some extent. The new Army Commander Lt Gen Maharaj Shri Rajendrasinhji, DSO, started enlarging on the original concept of POLO. The fresh overall plans included a slight increase in the number of troops to be employed, subsidiary operations on the border to make the opposition disperse its forces and an increase in the air support to be provided. The details of this intensification of the plan are described elsewhere. There was no change however in the role of 1 Armd Div which remained what it always had been, the capture of Hyderabad City from the West in the shortest time possible. Certain other troops were however allotted, the most important of these being 1 HORSE now temporarily equipped with Stuart tanks and one battery of 40 Med Regt.

Training up to date had been confined to unit training and the training of HQ only. Div HQ itself had not gone out as a whole, while the formation commanders, particularly the Divisional Commander, required practice in commanding their formations under active service conditions. It became apparent that with inexperienced staff officers and commanders, unless the Division was got together and a collective exercise held for a period of at least 5 days, the officers and men would not be able to visualise how the Armd Div worked together. Also, they would be unfamiliar with the many administrative problems that confronted a Division in operations. It was decided to hold a six-day exercise using all available troops and designed to test out command and staff at all levels, as well as battle procedure, administration, grouping and communications. As a result exercise " TUSKER " organized and run by the Armd Div Staff was carried out from the 5 to 11 July.

9 Inf Bde still being in Bangalore and as yet not under command of 1 Armd Div, the exercise was confined to 1 Armd Bde, 7 Inf Bde and Div troops. The country selected was similar to that which would be encountered in the move from Sholapur to Hyderabad, while the distance which the Division had to move during the exercise, was also the same as it would be for the operations. All vehicles except certain tracked vehicles took part. To save track mileage the armoured regiments

took out only a small percentage of light tanks to simulate the medium tanks. Except for the concentration period and the first day of the exercise, the weather was bad throughout. The monsoon was in full swing by this time. Though this bad weather proved uncomfortable to the participants, naturally the value gained by having to work in all types of weather was immense. Further, the knowledge gained in the crossing of small and large nalas in flood was alone worth the discomfort. The experience obtained from the exercise as a whole was of the greatest value to all concerned. Certain major lessons were re-emphasised, the chief of these concerning grouping, movement, and the absolute necessity for perfect MT and wireless discipline. The reiteration of these lessons were of the greatest help to all and particularly the Divisional Commander and his staff in the preparation of the final plan.

CHAPTER II.

"The First Contact."

Chapter I carried us on to 11 July and described the concentration period but for Chapter II the reader must go back one month. The law and order situation in Hyderabad, provoked mainly by the Razakars, had been deteriorating fast and Indian Union Police and Civil officials found themselves unable to cope with the raids that had started up from the Hyderabad side of the border. As a result, orders were received from Southern Command on 11 June that under instructions from the Government of India, any available Indian Army units stationed nearby were to move up to the border. From here they were to co-operate extremely closely with the police and assist them in every way to deal with raiders from Hyderabad territory, even if necessary, following the raiders into the State. Another reason for the move of troops up to the border areas, was to restore confidence among the local population who were fast becoming panicky. 1 Armd Div was allotted the border districts of Ahmednagar, Sholapur, Bijapur and Dharwar which meant a stretch of border extending over 400 miles. For these operations 9 Inf Bde less one battalion (1 BIHAR) at last came under command and moved from Bangalore to the Bijapur and Dharwar districts. As border protection meant splitting up into small parties and getting ready to play 'tag' across the frontier if necessary, the whole operation was given the code name KABADDI by the Division. The districts allotted were divided into three sectors on a road communications basis and each brigade was allotted a sector. The Armd Bde based on Ahmednagar was on the northern flank, 7 Inf Bde based on Poona and Sholapur was in the centre, while 9 Inf Bde based on Bijapur was on the southern flank.

As will be seen from the preceding Chapter, while operation KABADDI was being put into force, training had still to continue. The Divisional plan for KABADDI therefore utilised the minimum number of troops with the maximum possible deployment. Only a total of three and a half battalions and two troops of tanks were employed. Firm battalions bases were established at strategic communication centres, forward of these bases mobile company bases were established and a system of intensive patrolling in conjunction with the police, from these points was devised. Battalions were frequently changed so as to allow training to go on and in the first instance, apart from HQ 9 Inf Bde moving to Bijapur, other HQ remained where they were. Although the Government of India had given permission to follow up raiders into Hyderabad territory, this permission was not delegated below a Lt Col's command. In actual fact the border was never violated by Indian troops in any way except to cross over into Indian Union enclaves situated a few miles within Hyderabad territory and this only after giving prior warning to the Hyderabad Government. Later it became necessary to establish firm bases within these Indian Union enclaves and sub-units were then posted at Jamkhed and at Barsi. A look at the map will give the complexity of the border line, a relic of the feudal system.

Patrolling in aid of civil power continued with much sound but no fury until 24 July when the whole situation became extremely tense as a result of the Nanaj incident. On 24 July at 0845 hrs one company of 2 R SIKH while proceeding on a normal patrol from Sholapur to the large Indian Union enclave of Barsi and as such, after giving due warning, passing through a few miles of Hyderabad territory, were suddenly ambushed and heavily fired at from prepared positions just outside Nanaj village. The leading vehicle of the convoy came under automatic and small arms fire and a certain number of serious casualties were caused in the first few minutes. Fortunately the CO, Lt Col Prithipal Singh, happened to be accompanying this convoy on a tour of inspection. He immediately took control of the situation. The company was deployed and the hostiles in Nanaj were attacked. Another company of this battalion located at Barsi was called up by radio telephony and very soon moved down to the North of the village from where they also took concerted action. Within three hours the village had been captured and the 2 R SIKH firmly established. The casualties suffered by the Indian Army during this small engagement had been 1 JCO and 5 other ranks killed and 6 other ranks wounded. All these casualties had occurred within the first ten minutes. Casualties inflicted on the hostiles were about 50 killed. From a subsequent study of the position it was quite apparent that a deliberate ambush had been laid. The culprits were Pathans and Razakars while the State police was obviously involved. Later investigation showed that this was another case of indiscipline of the Razakars. They had cleared out the peaceful villagers, taken over control and were determined to precipitate an incident. This deliberate ambush of Indian Union troops engaged in their normal duties had an extremely sharp effect. Orders were received to occupy Nanaj permanently and, as a precautionary measure against further trouble of this kind, 7 Inf Bde less one battalion and 1 HORSE were moved to Sholapur as a reserve.

THE NANAJ INCIDENT

A view from the Block House prepared by the Razakars.

THE NANAJ INCIDENT

The Block House showing loopholes.

Shortly after this incident two other incidents followed in quick succession. In the northern portion of the Divisional sector at Khare Takli on the 27 July a column operating from Ahmednagar received information that 200 Razakars were preparing to attack a village in Indian territory. The column commander quickly moved his column on this report and on arrival at Khare Takli was fired at from across the border. Upon this he moved his forces which consisted only of 6 Stuart tanks right up to the border. By a short and well thought out encircling movement 35 armed hostiles were rounded up, who included three Sub-Inspectors and 16 other personnel of the Hyderabad police. Here again both the Razakars and State Police were involved.

Again on 5 August in the southern half of the sector at Hadalgi, two companies of 1 BIHAR, which had moved up to Sholapur by this time and were patrolling in this area, were fired at when going across to an Indian Union enclave. The fire came from the village of Yelasangi which is in Hyderabad territory. The column after some delay attacked the hostiles in Yelasangi and killed 62 Razakars and Pathans. Reinforcements which had been called up arrived later that night. Next morning however, all troops were withdrawn from Hyderabad territory and normal patrolling was resumed.

The implementation of operation KABADDI had meant of course, that 1 Armd Div already dispersed had become even more dispersed. Though this dispersion had been controlled by employing a minimum number of troops and making the best use of mobility, it is fair to say that the Division by the end of July was dispersed over an area of 4,000 square miles. At Appx 'A' is a location statement as on 31 July showing the grouping of all units within the Division.

The object of operation KABADDI had been to restore confidence among the civilian population as well as to assist the police in preventing violation of Indian territory by Hyderabad nationals. This object appeared to have been achieved. The closest liaison was maintained with the civil authorities in the districts and under orders from Div HQ it was incumbent on all formation and unit commanders taking part, to take the initiative in contacting their opposite numbers in the civil and police. The districts in which troops started to operate were ones which had seldom seen the Indian Army before. At first there was the usual suspicion between civil and military officers but this was very quickly overcome, presumably because of the orders which had been given to the troops to make the first overtures of friendship. As liaison became more and more closely established, it was most heartening to see how the civil and police officials as well as the villagers took the Army completely to their hearts and made much of them. Nothing was too much trouble to ensure that the troops were given the maximum help possible in anything that they wanted.

CHAPTER III.

"The Concentration."

On 5 August the newspapers in India had banner headlines of a story from Hyderabad. Apparently the Nanaj incident had created a crisis within the State. The Hyderabad Cabinet was divided, Gen El-Edroos was reported to have tendered his resignation and the whole situation was reported to be very fluid. The Government of India thinking that intervention in Hyderabad, if only to protect Indian nationals and property, would become immediately necessary owing to this crisis within the State, ordered the movement of all troops to their concentration areas.

There is no doubt that the crisis in Hyderabad had been a serious one. Kasim Razvi had apparently ordered the State Army to retake Nanaj. The Army had prevaricated. This had made the Razakars even more bellicose than they were before and while not willing to fight the Indian troops themselves, they took a vicarious revenge on the non-Muslim population. Bands of Razakars stationed all over the State increased their high-handed activities. Harmless passengers were pulled out of trains, searched and robbed. Stores were commandeered from private individuals to feed this voracious mob. Free medical treatment, food supplies and of course money, was demanded at the point of the gun. The worst act however was the molestation of women. No non-Muslim woman, whether in the city or whether in the districts dared venture forth when these hooligans were nearby. The State Police, despite a token show occasionally of attempting to restore normality, were obviously hand-in-glove with the miscreants. Orders seen after the Police Action show the close co-operation between the Razakars and the Police. An extract from a district Police order reads as follows: "I can send you no policemen but am sending you twenty Razakars." An excerpt from a civil officer's diary records how Razakars and Police burnt a Hindu village which had been "recalcitrant," with the civil officer looking on. To those who might think the situation has been exaggerated, it is only necessary to see the records that exist, to take the testimony of officials and to hear the views of non-partisan non-officials such as the European Missionaries. It would be unfair to say that all the officials were backing the Razakars in their misdeeds but there is no doubt that a large majority were, both from desire and a wish to show zeal and so ensure promotion. Of those who disagreed, the greater proportion kept silent with their heads buried in the sands of discretion, while the brave few resigned. Even the Nizam himself, still possessed of absolute power, was apparently aghast at this monster his ministers had created. If he tried to put them down now, perhaps they would turn and crush him. The ministers themselves, while still negotiating, were emptying the treasury, to the extent of 12 crores of rupees in one year, in keeping alive this organization and the adjuncts that went with it and their policy.

At 0900 hrs on 6 August the Divisional Commander was sent for by HQ Southern Command and asked to concentrate the Division at Sholapur by 1800 hrs on 10 August. According to the original plans the time allowed for concentration had been seven days, now it had to be done in four. Southern Command promised all help that they could give but asked the Division to make out their own movement orders. The move was to be by road and rail but the limiting factor as regards the rail moves was the provision of MBFUs to carry the Sherman tanks down by rail from Ahmednagar to Sholapur. Though dispersion had made training and other connected problems difficult, when it came to a question of movement, this very dispersion made a quick move easy. Three separate movement group commanders were nominated and each was given certain general instructions as to when and how to move. The details of the move were left to them. The sector commanders detailed were Brig S. D. Verma in Ahmednagar who was responsible for moving 1 Armd Bde and attached troops, Brig Apji Randhir Singh in Bijapur who was responsible for moving 9 Inf Bde and attached troops and Div HQ in Poona who were responsible for moving all troops in Poona. Div HQ also exercised general control over all movements. Road space on the sector Temburni-Sholapur which was common to the troops moving from Ahmednagar and from Poona was allotted by Div HQ and a control post was established at Temburni under the GSO 2— Maj R. D. Law. All convoys from the North and West were ordered to stage at Temburni for the night. Small advance parties in vehicles were despatched at 1600 hrs on the same day as the movement was ordered, that is 6 August and were instructed to arrive at Sholapur on 7 August. The camp at Sholapur had been previously reconnoitred and staff officers knew to which areas the various units in the formations should go.

The general plan for the move of the main bodies was that all B vehicles would go by road as well as those A vehicles which could be carried on transporters. The remainder would move by rail. Movement commenced according to plan but though the majority of the Division had got in by the time stipulated, certain small sections did not arrive till 12 August. The reason for this delay was the extremely bad weather which started up immediately the move was ordered. It must be remembered that the monsoon was in full swing by this time. Heavy rain caused spates in many of the nalas, the roads had Irish bridges which became unfordable while the road surface became extremely slippery. These were the main causes of the delay. Units arriving in Sholapur found that the original camp sites selected for them had by reason of the rain become untenable. Heavy rain combined with the black cotton soil made the ground almost impassable for wheels and so the first thing units had to do on arrival was to find new sites as well as dig, dig, dig.

Great credit must be given here to Sholapur (Indep) Sub-Area and its commander Brig S. N. Bhatia. Their arrangements at Sholapur both for the road and rail convoys were excellent. In filthy weather they were out at all hours of the day and night. Hot tea, meals and guides greeted all arrivals and it made no difference when they arrived. It was an example of thoroughly efficient staff work and the Armd Div were justly grateful.

As fate would have it, by the time the concentration was completed the excitement in Hyderabad was apparently dying down. The Commander of the Hyderabad State Forces had not resigned while the Hyderabad Cabinet seemed united again. Various sources in the State and in India, both official and non-official, rightly kept trying to facilitate negotiations. It became more and more apparent that the Division might have to remain at Sholapur far longer than the week that had originally been contemplated in the concentration plan. The biggest bugbear was the sanitary arrangements which had been made on the assumption that troops concentrating would only be remaining for a week. As the week started to increase, they were found to be most inadequate. This, though unpleasant at the time, was a lesson in itself. Units had to move well out of the original sites to camps at good distances from each other. As a result troops practised the art of bivouacking and also had plenty of room for themselves and for any local training that they wanted to do. It was good training to turn these minor misfortunes to some practical use.

As soon as this concentration started, 1 Armd Div asked HQ Southern Command for permission to reduce their KABADDI commitments. The concentration had achieved the " getting together " that had been wanting for some time and now was the final opportunity to train as a complete formation. If KABADDI in its original concept was not modified, there would still be considerable dispersion which apart from anything else, would cause a considerable delay in case a very quick entry into Hyderabad was ordered. Southern Command agreed with this appreciation and reduced 1 Armd Div's commitments to the Barsi enclave, the Nanaj garrison and down to only a few miles South of Sholapur. What was given up, was taken over by Bombay Area.

By this time of course 1 Armd Div's plans for the capture of Hyderabad City had matured considerably and training continued so as to prepare units and formations for the specific parts they were to play in these plans. The method used was the well tried one of holding a sand model discussion first and then doing the same exercise with troops on the ground that resembled as closely as possible the actual ground. Night operations and movement by night were constantly practised and certain specific exercises were also rehearsed. These included:—

> (a) The capture of a bridge by night and prevention of its demolition by the enemy;
> (b) Capture of enemy gun positions by night; and
> (c) Capture and clearing of large villages manned by regulars and irregulars.

These exercises proved to be of the most immense value in the subsequent operations that followed.

A word must be said on morale. By this time, of course, morale was as high as possible. The concentration, the training together, the complete equipping and the prospect of action in the immediate future were the main contributory causes. This high morale was sedulously fostered. By various means the spirit of comradeship was built up and a Divisional esprit-de-corps, so essential in a formation, came into being. In the Division what little crime there had been, dropped to nil and the simple threat of "All right, I'll send you away on leave," was enough to ensure exemplary behaviour. On 23 August the Army Commander visited the troops and the state of training and morale in the Division can best be summed up by the text of a signal he sent to the Division on his return to Poona. This read:—

> "I wish to congratulate you and the troops under your command for the magnificent showing I noticed. everywhere on my visit yesterday. It is seldom that one is privileged to see a force which combines friendliness, contentedness, efficiency and confidence. You had them all, no wonder your morale stands high."

CHAPTER IV

Part I—"The Appreciation"

Information regarding the strength, dispositions and intentions, of the regular and irregular forces of Hyderabad, was now being regularly received, but, as in all operations the reliability of such information was very much under question. The main sources of information were of course the files with the Military Adviser-in-Chief, Indian State Forces. This information, which was somewhat out of date, was supplemented by information received from agents, wireless intercepts, travellers and the so-called State Congress sources. Agents being untrained, were both inaccurate and unreliable but their unreliability was as nothing compared to State Congress sources, whose reports were the most highly exaggerated, inaccurate and full of personal propaganda that any army has ever received. Wireless intercepts were useful in finding out moves, possible intentions and the state of training and here credit must be given to 1 Armd Div Signal Regt for organising the intercept service for Southern Command and breaking down the Hyderabad code in use. This intercept group was kept on at Div HQ throughout the operations and was of the greatest value at all times. Lastly, the travellers were full of tales but were useful in helping to confirm other tales. While facts gleaned from these various sources were being collated, HQ Southern Command got a windfall in the shape of a really reliable "informer" who visited them from Hyderabad. This man, though prone to exaggeration like all others, gave fairly accurately the strength, dispositions and plans of the Hyderabad Armed Forces, in the event of military action by India.

From a review of all this information, the picture of Hyderabad State's armed strength appeared to be

Regular Army	22,000	Armed with modern weapons incl 8 25-pr guns and three regts of armd cars.
Irregular troops	10,000	About 25 per cent armed with modern small arms, remainder with muzzle loaders.
Armed Arabs, Paigah Forces, etc.	10,000	As above.

Armed Police, Customs Forces	10,000 ..	Armed with modern rifles and Stens only.
Razakars	.. 2,00,000	About 20 per cent armed with modern small arms, the remainder with muzzle loaders, spears, swords, etc.

At the end of operations, when figures from Hyderabad records became available, the above estimations were found to be fairly accurate.

The early moves by Indian troops to their concentration areas, combined with the appalling lack of security sense among junior officers and civilians connected with the operations, as well as the agents the State obviously had, made it quite apparent to the Hyderabad High Command as to where the main attacks were coming from and roughly what their weight would be.

On the Indian Union side, the strategy that Hyderabad would employ was thought to be either

> (a) An attempt to hold our troops on the borders of Hyderabad with selected units and to make extensive use of demolitions in slowing up the advance. Combined with this, attacks on the line of communication by guerilla forces
>
> or
>
> (b) To allow penetration until the columns had reached to within fifty miles of Hyderabad City and then to attack them and their extended lines of communication with all forces available.

In both cases the use of an extensive fifth column, delaying tactics such as poisoning wells and damaging communications, plus the creation of a huge refugee problem to hamper troop movements was to be expected. Another major factor to be considered was of course the probable fanaticism of Muslims fighting a Jehad.

Opinion was divided as to what might be Hyderabad's strategy after Hyderabad City had been occupied. One school of thought considered that any armed forces remaining, whether regular or irregular, would disperse, intent on carrying out guerilla warfare and the massacre of Hindus until finally rounded up. Another school considered that even on the threat of Hyderabad City being captured, the State Forces would capitulate, though Razakars might try guerilla tactics for some short time.

The vigorous and bombastic propaganda that the Hyderabad publicity machine had built up, was of course confusing thought among amateur strategists to an alarming degree. Some said that the Hyderabad Forces would open a corridor to Portuguese Goa and reinforcements from Muslim countries with arms would come through here. Others said that Bezwada on the East, Ahmednagar and Sholapur to the West and Bellary to the South would be invaded. Kasim Razvi's speech, in which he said that the waters of the Indian Ocean would lap the feet of the Nizam's throne, added credence to these thoughts. Others spoke of mass Muslim uprisings in South India, particularly among the Moplahs, while the talk of a violent Muslim uprising in India was a commonplace. To the informed and those who both understood and considered the situation, the majority of such ideas were of course the purest fancy. The State Army would not be able to force corridors, troops from Muslim countries would not be able to come to the direct aid of Hyderabad; while in India itself the tenor of the Indian Muslims had clearly shown their disagreement with Hyderabad's policy. Unfortunately such balanced minds were in the minority. A large group of people, particularly those who were against the idea of armed intervention in Hyderabad, made much capital out of such ideas.

Opinions varied as to what air forces Hyderabad could produce on her own. It was not known what aircraft she had in the State suitable for use in a military role. Obviously she could not have many, if any at all. Agents' reports here were really fantastic and their reports always described one Tiger Moth as a squadron of modern fighters. Aircraft were also thought to have been purchased in the West and located in Pakistan, which on D day would be flown to Hyderabad. This was in fact, a possible danger but much minimised by the knowledge that there was obviously no proper base organisation available in Hyderabad for military aircraft.

What part Pakistan would play in such armed intervention was, of course, of the greatest interest. This was the one factor which it was not possible to gauge accurately. Looking at it purely from a soldier's personal point of view, it was obvious that Pakistan ground forces could undertake no direct intervention in Hyderabad. They were already engaged in Kashmir and the best they could do was attack India's western frontier. This would mean war between the two Dominions. With regard to air support, one look at the map clearly indicated that Pakistan bombers could not intervene in Hyderabad from bases in Pakistan, while no ground organisation existed within the State to base bombers there. Fighter cover for such bombers was out of the question owing to range. Goa was again mentioned as being a suitable air base and yet it was known to have no proper airfield. The possible attacking of India by Pakistan in the event of military action in Hyderabad was again made much of by those who did not want such military action.

Propaganda was also put about, that Hyderabad or Pakistan based aircraft, would not only attack the advancing Indian Forces but would also bomb big cities like Bombay, Poona, Madras and even Delhi. This propaganda certainly seemed to cause a certain amount of alarm among the Provincial Governments concerned while large numbers of rich but timid merchants evacuated their families and themselves to the districts.

Confusion was even more confounded by the figure of Sidney Cotton. It soon became apparent that this middle-aged and tough Australian, had a concern with bases in Europe and Pakistan, which was engaged in aerial gun-running into Hyderabad. While this fact was known to the Government of India, owing to the huge distances involved and the lack of Radar facilities, interception was not possible. As the matter became more public, Cotton became more blatant and even admitted that he was flying into Hyderabad. He described his actions however as " mercy " flights, designed solely to carry medicines and other urgent necessities of life. In actual fact his cargo was arms. The flights were made usually by night and Bidar, later Warangal, were the receiving airfields. It was difficult to check the number of flights made or the quantities of arms brought in. Reports as usual were exaggerated. There was also the possibility that the Cotton aircraft, which were known to be Lancasters, would be used in a bombing role. It was later discovered that these gun-running sorties had brought in only a few arms, the details of which are given in Appx B. The whole business had really solely benefited in a big financial way, Cotton himself and his Hyderabadi, Pakistani and European confederates. Hyderabad had not benefited to anywhere near the extent of the money paid and at the end of the operations, all Cotton's arms were taken over by the Indian Army.

In the midst of all this loose thinking about Hyderabad's possible might, mainly induced, no doubt, by good and loud propaganda, three important points were missed by many. These were:—

(a) The temperament of the Deccani Mussalman,

(b) The lack of modern experience and training in the Hyderabad Army,

and

(c) The experience and personality of the Military Commander.

In 1932, Deccani Muslim recruitment into the Indian Army was stopped, as their quality and physical stamina had started to go right down. During the 1939-1945 War, owing to the increase of man power, enlistment was again opened to this class but only to the ancillary services. Also in this War some Hyderabad State Forces had gone out of India, it is true, but those that had escaped being captured without a shot being fired in Malaya, had only been employed on the Lines of Communication.

Equipment held was not new and was badly maintained. Hyderabadi officers and NCOs were on the whole badly trained and conditions in the State did not always ensure that the most efficient were promoted. Commanders and staffs were ill trained, while cliques mitigated against that homogeneity that is so essential in any army.

At the head of this army and consequently also adviser with regard to irregulars, Razakars and Arabs was the Commander, Major-General Syed Ahmed El-Edroos. The presence and personality of this Commander, was without doubt, a factor which played a large part in the estimates that were made of Hyderabad's armed strength. Born of Arab stock, that had migrated to the State three generations before, and had since then continuously served the Nizam in his army, Edroos was a figure that certainly influenced Hyderabad's decision. Though outwardly impressive, lack of opportunity had not given him the experience, that he should have had as a Commander. While popular with some, particularly foreigners because of his good social manner, a streak of intolerance and misjudged ruthlessness made his subordinates fear him. As a result, he was neither able to gain their confidence nor receive from them the advice and true representation of facts that he should have had. His lack of experience and training, possibly through no fault of his own, made him misjudge the capabilities of his troops. While disdaining to be a politician, this very disdain made him an easy prey to their machinations. A combination of all these factors made him appreciate wrongly the worth of his own troops and certainly that of the Indian Forces. As a result, the advice he gave his ruler and Government was incorrect, while his lack of political acumen allowed him to be pushed into situations which were untenable. In defeat however his good qualities came to the fore. He retained to the end a soldier's code of honour in dealing with other soldiers, while his obvious concern for his troops, when his eyes were opened to the hopelessness of the struggle, was a major factor in the reasons for an early capitulation. His attitude when surrendering his army was dignified and correct. His willing and unreserved co-operation after the surrender, in the face of much calumny by his own people, did much to win him the respect of the soldiers of the Indian Union and the fair and just treatment he received from them was certainly earned by his behaviour. A certain criticism has been made by uninformed persons of his continued retention at the head of the State Army after the surrender. The main reason was that there was no one else in the Hyderabad Army, capable of assuming that position.

Though El-Edroos had told his ruler and ministers, that he could " slash " any attacks by the Indian Army for three months, in fact the Hyderabad Army was banking on the Indian Union being incapable of any action at all, because of its preoccupation in Kashmir and on an

Internal Defence role. They further thought that if there was any action, it would be so weak and so ineptly led, that it could be stopped by the forces disposed near the borders. Their estimate of our strength was grossly underrated. Not more than 60 tanks were envisaged while the number of guns was estimated at about 16. 50 per cent of B vehicles were thought to be " off road " while the opinion left by retiring British officers " that once they left, the Indian Army would be without leaders of any calibre " was widely believed. The term most commonly used about the Indian Union Forces was " that bania army." On the Hyderabad side, propaganda and the disinclination to look facts fairly in the face had given them an exaggerated idea of their own and the Razakar potential. Lack of training and possibly sheer laziness, had prevented what plan there was being either accurate or in any detail. Administration, so essential in war but so difficult and arduous a task to perfect, had been left almost untouched. What there was of it was ' ad hoc.'

Very briefly, the Hyderabad plan as far as an Indian Union advance from Sholapur (1 Armd Div axis) was concerned, consisted of

(a) a strong stop on the line Naldrug and Tuljapur
(b) a defensive position in the Talmud defile
(c) a brigade position on the Zahirabad-Bidar line, and
(d) a really strong mined entrenched position at Sangareddipet-Patancheru, if of course, the Indian Forces were allowed to get that far.

Combined with this there was to be active Razakar and Irregular action against the long lines of communication, supported and stiffened by newly raised " territorial " and " refugee " battalions from the Gulbarga area. The putting into action of this plan and how it worked, out is described later.

Part II—" The 1 Armd Div Plan "

The object of 1 Armd Div had always been to advance as quickly as possible along the road Sholapur-Hyderabad with the intention of capturing and occupying Hyderabad City. With the resources available and with the need for having strong forces concentrated for use in the City and outskirts, no large diversions were possible. In this object, however, Southern Command had ordered that Bidar airfield 24 miles off the main road be captured, so that air support which would have been based at a considerable distance from the scene of operations, could move up to Bidar for the last phases. After the capture of Hyderabad City however, the troops were to fan out to all parts of Hyderabad State to clear the expected guerilla opposition, to put down looting and rioting and to re-establish normal conditions as quickly as possible.

Exercise 'TUSKER' had shown that it was not possible when using a single road, for the Armd Div to move together as a whole and that if proper replenishment, particularly of POL, was to be done, then at least one quarter of the Division would have to be immobile at any one time. Without halting this one quarter, road space would not permit the movement of administrative echelons. Exercise 'TUSKER' had also re-emphasised the advantage of self-contained groups moving in support of each other and designed with either a preponderance of tanks or a preponderance of infantry so that they could be switched and used for the best purpose as the situation demanded. Successful grouping based on the opposition expected was essential and after some thought the forces operating under the command of 1 Armd Div were divided into five groups and, for ease of reference, security as well as the denoting of their particular role, certain code names were given to them. These groups were:—

(a) STRIKE FORCE—commanded by Lt Col Ram Singh. This was to be a small mobile force of all arms acting in the advanced guard role and intended to move quickly, seize tactical points and to brush aside minor opposition.

(b) SMASH FORCE—commanded by Brig S. D. Verma. This was the main armoured column with two regiments of armour plus the SP artillery, the medium guns and two battalions of infantry. Their main role was naturally the armoured role but in the event of a set piece infantry attack they could support it very strongly.

(c) KILL FORCE—commanded by Brig Gurbachan Singh. This consisted of 7 Inf Bde Group together with a certain amount of artillery which included the one battery of the A Tk Regt available but less one of their battalions which had been moved to SMASH FORCE. This was one of the two main infantry forces.

(d) VIR FORCE—commanded by Brig Apji Randhir Singh. This consisted of 9 Inf Bde Group complete. This was the second of the main infantry groups.

(e) REAR DIV—under this heading were grouped all the administrative units and details that were not required forward for operations. Under command however, were put certain fighting sub-units, consisting of one squadron 1 HORSE and one battery of 26 LAA Regt for the static protection of Rear Div and the protection of administrative echelons on the move.

It was made quite clear, that under all circumstances, each group was responsible for its own local protection. This edict covered Rear Div as well.

NALDRUG

Aerial view of the Naldrug Bridge.

As infantry and armour were to work so closely together and a certain confusion had been noticed during training regarding the nomenclature of administrative echelons, for this operation, all units and formations were ordered to classify their vehicles into three echelons.

(a) F echelon to consist of A and B fighting vehicles and guns.

(b) B echelon to consist of the minimum number of administrative soft vehicles which were required either with or near F echelon, and

(c) D echelon to consist of vehicles considered non-essential during the first phase of operations, that is, about one week.

The importance of reducing to a bare minimum the number of vehicles taken forward was constantly emphasised and all vehicles in D echelon were relegated to and moved with Rear Div, under their direct command.

At Appx C is given the detailed lay out of the groups mentioned above.

As has been stated before, the whole intention of 1 Armd Div's advance was to reach Hyderabad City as soon as possible. The first stand from the Hyderabad Forces was expected to be along the line Naldrug-Tuljapur, a line running at right-angles to the axis of advance, while Naldrug itself, on the main road was tactically most important. It was obviously essential to secure Naldrug extremely quickly and effectively, thus making a good start for the operations. This capture would also secure the one bottleneck en route—the bridge over the river at Naldrug. This bridge was possibly the most important point in the minds of the 1 Armd Div planners when possible operations were being worked out. High, narrow, long and vulnerable, the Naldrug bridge carried the road over the river Bori. Owing to the monsoon prevalent at the time, the river was in flood and would be fordable only with difficulty. Eye-witness reports stated that the bridge was closely guarded by the Hyderabad Forces while it was also reliably stated to have been prepared for demolition. If this bridge was blown up by the defenders, then much delay would occur in crossing this obstacle and moving forward to Hyderabad. This delay would definitely prejudice surprise and would give time for the movement of reinforcements westwards from Hyderabad. In fact the whole plan for the capture of Naldrug really centred about the capture of the bridge intact. Once the bridge had been captured, quick forward movement could take place by tanks, while the supply problem would certainly become much easier.

In bare essentials, the plan of 1 Armd Div was as follows:

KILL FORCE (7 Inf Bde Group) was to move up to Naldrug from the South under cover of darkness and seize the bridge intact. As a subsidiary to this operation they were also to occupy the village of Jalkot, where it was suspected that a battery of 25-pr guns was located. Once these objectives had been gained, road blocks were to be established East of Naldrug to prevent movement of Hyderabadi reinforcements along this road. These operations by KILL FORCE were to be carried out by night and the objectives were to be secured by 0400 hrs on D day. No motor transport was allowed to KILL FORCE during this phase. Their transport was to be brigaded and moved up to them later when road space became available. Permission was given however that a minimum number of bullock carts and donkeys could be hired, to move wireless sets and mortar ammunition, etc, during the night advance. In granting this permission, a minor consideration also was that in the event of the battalion groups losing their way, the bullock and donkey drivers recruited locally, might be able to act as guides.

SMASH FORCE (1 Armd Bde Group) was to advance down the main road to Naldrug, leaving their concentration areas by 0400 hrs and crossing the border at 0430 hrs. This timing meant two hours night driving by the tanks, which were naturally in the lead. In view of the fact that by 0400 hrs the need for surprise would have diminished due to the action being taken by KILL FORCE, headlights were allowed to every third tank. Before 1 Armd Bde moved, a small subsidiary operation by part of their infantry component was to be executed, to capture a small enemy post located on the main road East of Naldrug at the village of Itkal, 3 miles from the border. This was also to be cleared by 0400 hrs. The arrival of the leading tanks at Naldrug was timed for 0600 hrs, by which time there would be enough light to let the tank gunners shoot. Once at Naldrug, 1 Armd Bde were to take on any enemy that they encountered, to occupy and search the town with their infantry and to exploit to Jalkot and a further 2 miles, if possible, in support of 7 Inf Bde Group. They were also to block the exits from Naldrug northwards and southwards with the dual purpose of ensuring no forces escaped, as well as the prevention of reinforcements coming in from either of these two directions.

If the bridge had been blown, 1 Armd Bde was to find a ford over the river and to move some tanks across as soon as possible, primarily to support 7 Inf Bde in case any enemy armour had moved down the road from the East. 1 Armd Bde's artillery and tank gun targets had been very carefully worked out in conjunction with 7 Inf Bde, so that neither group would shoot up the other. This co-ordination, which was difficult but essential, worked most satisfactorily.

If the bridge was intact and preliminary exploitation as well as reports from 7 Inf Bde showed no enemy concentrations East of Naldrug, on orders from HQ 1 Armd Div, 1 Armd Bde was to clear the road of all vehicles. STRIKE FORCE, which in the plan, would by this time have been moved up to just behind 1 Armd Bde, were then to be pushed through as quickly as possible with the intention of exploiting as far forward as Umerga and in fact occupying the town by that evening. This would achieve on the first day a quick penetration of about 28 miles. In case the bridge was blown up, a bridging column had been got together and located off the road well forward during the concentration. Instead of STRIKE FORCE, this column was to move up immediately behind 1 Armd Bde to throw a Bailey bridge across the broken spans as soon as possible.

VIR FORCE (9 Inf Bde Group) were to act in a subsidiary role to this main operation. Their orders were to capture Tuljapur by a dawn operation, establish 1 MEWAR Inf there and then move eastwards along the road Tuljapur-Lohara protecting the left flank of the main attack. From Lohara they were to turn South and advance as far as Yenagur on the main axis, beyond which point they were not to pass, until such time as they were required forward or road space was given to them under orders from Div HQ. This subsidiary operation was part of the overall Southern Command plan and designed to give an impetus to the " probing " operations by Bombay Area along the border. It was useful to 1 Armd Div in that it protected their northern flank, prevented the enemy breaking North from Naldrug and also saved road space on the main axis. Once operations started and Tuljapur had been captured, all border operations were to come under HQ Bombay Area and were no longer to be the concern of 1 Armd Div.

Rear Div Group was to remain concentrated at Sholapur, ready to make its first bound to Naldrug once this was clear. This was not to be before D plus 1 day.

The salient points of the plan were an attempt to achieve complete surprise, to capture the Naldrug bridge intact, to strike any opposition a really hard initial blow and to penetrate as deeply as possible into Hyderabad territory—all on the first day of operations. It was felt that all this would have the most effective repercussions on the morale of the Hyderabad Army which would thus make the task of our advancing forces much easier. As can be seen, the attack was also planned, so as to ensure that no reinforcements could reach Naldrug in case of a hold-up there owing to the bridge being destroyed, nor could the Naldrug garrison withdraw with their forces intact if such had been their orders.

The number of air sorties available was extremely limited while owing to the Tempests having to operate from Poona airfield, the time over the target was also short. Generally speaking, air support for the Divisional advance was limited to Tac R along the main road and all roads which led on to the main road. Aircraft were also asked to take on with rockets and cannons, any military transport moving on to the main road, westwards along the main road or eastwards into Hyderabad. In addition to RIAF air support the Divisional Air OP flight was given a subsidiary role when they were not actually firing the guns. This role was reporting back to Div HQ the progress made by the various columns of 1 Armd Div.

The time required to move to concentration areas for putting this plan into action needed a minimum of 48 hours. If the troops were moved to their final concentration areas and then kept there for any length of time, the whole plan would be given away and this point was emphasised very strongly. In fact, it was made quite clear that the move to concentration areas should not be ordered unless the Government of India was prepared to go ahead with the Police Action into Hyderabad. At Appx D and Appx E will be found the actual operation orders giving in detail the moves of formations to their concentration areas and the orders for the main attack on D day. Dependent on how operations went on D day, orders were to be issued each evening for the operations on succeeding days.

In the making of this plan, a deception cover plan to " mystify and mislead " the enemy was considered. The concentration and move of 7 Inf Bde Group to the South had been put about as a plan to attack Gulbarga. This impression was heightened by dummy aerial reconnaissances along the track and road Sholapur-Gulbarga as well as the execution of certain road repairs along this track. The concentration of part of 9 Inf Bde Group at Barsi, prior to their move South-East and attack on Tuljapur, was given out as an attack on Latur. To cover the noise of the tanks moving down the main road on D day and to " make familiar and contemptuous " the noise of such tanks to enemy outposts, ever since the Division had started to concentrate in Sholapur, small parties of tanks were as a matter of routine moved up to the border at night, told to make a noise with their engines and come back again at dawn.

It will be seen from the above, that any plans made, were made carefully and in great detail. At all stages of the Divisional planning, the brigade commanders concerned were consulted, while at the higher level planning at Southern Command, the Divisional Commander was kept well in the picture. The success of these operations is largely attributed to this detailed planning for which sufficient time was available, as well as the extremely pleasant and efficient atmosphere in which it was carried out at all levels. Matters were discussed, re-discussed and then discussed again. The result obtained was that not only did every commander at all levels know what he had to do but was also completely in his superior commander's mind and, therefore, capable of taking action along the right lines in case minor changes were necessary, as they invariably are, in any battle.

About the first week of September it seemed to be getting fairly apparent that the Indian Union would have to implement Police Action. On 10 September, the Divisional Commander suddenly called up to Poona for discussions with the Army Commander, was told that the operations were on. D day was left by Army HQ to HQ Southern Command and rightly so. It was unanimously agreed on 10 September, that Monday, 13 September, would be a suitable date. Questions have been asked later as to why this particular date was chosen and the questions have varied from "don't you think the 13th was an unlucky date" to "did you consult a pandit before choosing the date and the time." In actual fact 13 September was selected, because by that date concentrations could be completed with 24 hours in hand to spare in case the weather went wrong. The only pandits who were consulted, were military pandits in the shape of the Army Commander, the BGS and the Divisional Commander, who all agreed that if the Police Action was going to be put on, the sooner it was done the better. This speed of implementation was essential from the security point of view. It is interesting to note that Hyderabad got to hear rumours of this projected action by the Government of India through certain press agency sources. They were, however, convinced that 15 September was the date. Later, the Divisional Commander was told that even after D day had been decided on by those concerned as being 13 September, efforts had been made by interested parties to postpone it indefinitely or at any rate till 15 September.

CHAPTER V

Southern Command's Plan

This book has been written from the viewpoint of 1 Armd Div but before the day-to-day fortunes of 1 Armd Div are discussed, it is extremely necessary here to indicate briefly Southern Command's complete plan for operation 'POLO,' and the part played by other units and formations. This is also necessary so as to disabuse the mind of any reader who gets the impression that the operation was solely the responsibility of 1 Armd Div. In fact, it was anything but this. The Armoured Division was merely part of the whole integrated plan and much of its success was due to the successful and co-ordinated action taken by other units and formations.

The basic plan had envisaged two thrusts, a strong one from the West and a weaker one from the East. The thrust from the West was the responsibility of 1 Armd Div while the thrust from the East was put under the general command of HQ Madras Area, who subsequently gave operational control of the troops concerned to HQ Bezwada Sub-Area, which was formed for this purpose from HQ Madras Sub-Area. The actual troops taking part in this eastern thrust, which was to move along the road-axis Bezwada-Kodar-Suryapet-Hyderabad, consisted of the 2/5 RGR with under command one squadron of 17 HORSE, (Sherman tanks) lent from 1 Armd Div, and one battery of 25 pr. The command of this composite group was given to Lt Col Amrik Singh, MC, Commander 2/5 RGR. Instructions for this force were to advance along the main route up as far as within 30 miles of Hyderabad City, after which they were to come under command of HQ 1 Armd Div for further operations. A further advance was not ordered for them for various reasons, primarily the lack of knowledge as to what opposition might be met outside Hyderabad City and secondly, because of the necessity of having strong co-ordinated forces available when the City was entered. The thrust as such was completely successful and after meeting a certain amount of opposition, the troops arrived at Suryapet the day before the surrender occurred. Further advance might have been difficult owing to successful demolitions. The effect of this thrust was to drive the Hyderabad State Forces opposing them into the capital. Opposition was negligible, consisting mostly of panic-stricken retreating troops and some stauncher irregulars.

As regards other operations, the borders of Hyderabad had been divided into three sectors, the western sector under HQ Bombay Area, the northern sector under HQ Jubbulpore (Indep) Sub-Area and the eastern and southern sectors under HQ Madras Area. Available troops formed into small columns, were instructed to move forward along the various main roads leading into State territory. Their main tasks were the seizure and security of important road junctions, defiles and road and railway bridges. They were also to take over important civil centres and keep the administration going. Finally, they were to be responsible for the maintenance of law and order in the areas they occupied. In addition, HQ Bombay Area was given the most important task of capturing the second city of Hyderabad State—Aurangabad—a task that they achieved on D plus 2 day with complete success. This capture of Aurangabad had a material effect on the morale of the Hyderabad Government and the Hyderabad Army.

Great credit must be given to the HQ Areas concerned for the part they played in these operations. Troops put at their disposal were either single battalions or ad hoc columns found from sub-units, schools of instruction, etc. The administration of such forces was, as always, a major difficulty while the improvised wireless communications over the long distances involved was another handicap. The fact that these difficulties were overcome successfully, showed to a great extent the zeal, accuracy and enthusiasm with which the operations were planned and executed. Though penetration into Hyderabad territory was not deep, it was effective.

In addition to operations by the Military, the Indian Union Police along the Hyderabad borders were instructed to leave the main roads alone but to probe forward along tracks as far as they could with the limited resources available. They were specifically warned not to get embroiled in a pitched battle or to fight the Hyderabad State Forces. This probing forward by Police units was only partially successful and with their many limitations this was all that it could be.

The air plan, which was being directed by Air Vice Marshal S. Mukherjee, OBE, from Poona, where he was very closely in touch with the GOC-in-C, Southern Command, visualized close support for the operations from airfields at Poona and Gannavaram (Bezwada). The distance these airfields were away from the actual progress of operations, mitigated against the time aircraft could be over the target. Though a temporary airstrip had been built at Sholapur, at best it was only an emergency strip due to the monsoons. It was occasionally used by communications aircraft. The total strength of RIAF taking part was two weak fighter squadrons and the odd Dakota converted into an ad hoc bomber. As far as 1 Armd Div was concerned, the details of the air support they received have been given in the text. On the strategic level, the converted Dakota bombers were used on D day to neutralize all airfields within Hyderabad State, with the exception of Hakimpet and Begumpet airfields serving Hyderabad city. This neutralization was carried out extremely effectively.

CHAPTER VI

D DAY—13 SEP, 48

On 11 September while units were actually moving out to their concentration areas, news was received of Jinnah's death. Among the more senior officers, the effect of this news on future events was a matter of great speculation. Among the more junior officers and the troops, not much concern was felt and perhaps it would be fair to say that among some, the incident was thought to be a good omen. Orders were received from HQ Southern Command to fly flags at half mast and this was punctiliously observed.

By the morning of 12 September all troops were in their concentration areas but the final confirmation that operations were to take place on the 13 September was still to be received from HQ Southern Command. It had been agreed previously that this final confirmation would be passed over the secraphone by means of a personal call from the Army Commander to the Divisional Commander and that to save errors, no other method of confirmation could be accepted. It had been agreed that this confirmation would be given about midday. From 12 noon onwards the Divisional Commander sat impatiently in the office of the Commander, Sholapur (Indep) Sub-Area. He was aware of the plan and so was the Sub-Area Commander, but the many visitors who kept on dropping in, were not. Being a Sunday, there were a large number of visitors and visitors of all types. The local policeman dropped in and so did the District Magistrate. The Manager of one of the larger mills looked in to arrange about a conducted tour of troops round his mill on the following day. A number of junior officers from Sub-Area HQ came in to see what their seniors were doing, while the local Traffic Manager of the Railways wandered in to complain of an overdue goods train. All of them naturally wanted to know what the latest on Hyderabad was and a lot of good natured chaffing took place. Not one of them however realised how close H hour was, the secret, even in Sholapur, had been well kept. At about 1315 hrs the Divisional Commander, who by this time was most impatient, heaved a sigh of relief. The telephone was ringing and as he answered it, he received the OK from the Army Commander. Time had been available to work out plans carefully and all that was required to implement final orders was the issue of certain code words to formation commanders. By 1400 hrs on 12 September, all these code words had been sent out and acknowledged by those waiting to take part. As wireless silence had been imposed till 0300 hrs on D day, all that could be done at Div HQ was to sit in patience and wait until the first call came through. Every one was most cheerful, with a high morale and supremely confident of the success of operations.

The weather, which had been a variable factor in all planning, remained good. The night 12/13 September was clear with no clouds and there had been no rain for over 48 hours. Moonrise was not till very early in the morning of 13 September and even then the amount of light would be negligible. Climatic conditions, considering the time of year, could not have been better for the operations that were to take place.

Sequence of Operations

Operations by Kill Force (7 Inf Bde Gp).

It will be remembered that this Bde Gp had been given the following tasks:—

- (a) to capture intact the Naldrug bridge from the South,
- (b) to establish road blocks between Naldrug bridge and Jalkot with a view to preventing any military movement by the Hyderabad Forces on the main road, and
- (c) to destroy any enemy guns in or near the village of Jalkot.

3 IND GRS with under command a detachment of 65 Fd Coy, RIE, to remove any charges that had been placed on the bridge, had been given the task of capturing the Naldrug bridge. 2 R SIKH had been given the task of capturing Jalkot village, destroying any enemy guns there and establishing the road blocks required. These two groups moved off to time in separate columns, with Bde HQ following behind on the 3 IND GRS axis. The State border was crossed exactly on time and both battalions despite the darkness of the night, managed remarkably well to keep to the axis of advance that had been given them. The going proved to be far more difficult than had been anticipated and the rain-softened and undulating countryside did not assist in any way. The local guides with the bullock carts and donkeys proved to be a complete failure. In fact, in the final stages of the advance, these bullock carts had to be left behind as they could not keep up. Despite these difficulties, by 0400 hrs, 3 IND GRS, a little late on their schedule, were coming up to the Naldrug bridge. Their approach march was not observed and on arrival they found that though it had been prepared for demolition, no charges had actually been placed. 2 R SIKH had captured Jalkot village also about one hour later than schedule and found only one 25 pr gun there, which they captured without either it or they firing a round. By 0550 hrs, 7 Inf Bde appeared to have

secured its objectives and established strong road blocks in the area of the high ground near mile stones 154 and 153, about four miles East of Naldrug village.

Owing to the bullock carts not being able to keep up with the column, the delay due to indifferent going and the fact that wireless communication was extremely bad owing to atmospherics, no message from 7 Inf Bde Gp was received at Div HQ at 0400 hrs on D day as had been expected. In fact, when 1 Armd Bde started to move out, the whereabouts of 7 Inf Bde was not known.

Operations by Smash Force (1 Armd Bde Gp).

1 Armd Bde had been concentrated on the border behind the village of Tandulwadi on the main road Sholapur-Hyderabad. According to their plan, the leading element (17 HORSE) was to cross the border at 0400 hrs after the capture of Itkal by one company of 14 RAJPUT had been signalled. Bde Tac HQ moved to the starting point by 0330 hrs and waited for the success signal from the company of 14 RAJPUT due by 0345 hrs. At 0400 hrs no news had been received either from the company detailed to capture Itkal or from 7 Inf Bde about the capture of Naldrug bridge. The Brigade Commander, naturally a little perturbed, called up Div HQ on the R/T. A brief discussion ensued and realising what might have caused the delays the Divisional Commander ordered 1 Armd Bde to go ahead and be prepared to liquidate both Itkal and Naldrug with their tanks and infantry, in case the other operations had gone astray.

Though there was slight concern at Div HQ because of no signals having been received from 7 Inf Bde, there was no real worry. The difficulties of signal communications had been realised, possible delay owing to bad going over unreconnoitred country was allowed for, while the Divisional Commander himself was quite confident that 7 Inf Bde would get to their objective at the latest, by first light.

The leading elements of 1 Armd Bde were through Itkal by 0505 hrs and found that the company of 14 RAJPUT had done good work, having liquidated the Hyderabadi outpost killing approximately 16. Due to inexperience, the officer in charge finding a little shooting still going on, had hesitated to give the success signal and was still mopping up in the dark. Commander, 1 Armd Bde, decided to leave a troop of Stuart tanks to help this company in their task and the advance continued. By first light, 0545 hrs, leading elements of 17 HORSE had reached the dak-bungalow area overlooking Naldrug from the West. There was still no news from 7 Inf Bde nor, in the dim light, could they be seen across the river. In order not to cause casualties to 7 Inf Bde troops, fire was not opened on the Naldrug bridge area or to the East of the town. From the direction of Naldrug some hostile artillery fire was falling on the leading elements and small arms fire was also coming from the East and North East. There had been one or two casualties. The light, though still dim was improving as the sun came over the horizon and a careful forward reconnaissance disclosed that the bridge was still intact though whether the piers were damaged could not be seen. One squadron of Sherman tanks was ordered to avoid the bridge and reconnoitre a crossing over the river so as to get on to the East bank as quickly as possible. While this was being done, contact was made with 7 Inf Bde and the R/T came up strong and clear. Finding the bridge clear and contact with 7 Inf Bde Gp established, operations as previously planned started to move extremely quickly.

By 0830 hrs 17 HORSE, well across the river were advancing East along the road, contacting those elements of 7 Inf Bde who had made the road blocks and ready to act in their support if required. In Naldrug itself, 4 GWALIOR Inf, the unit that was to occupy Naldrug and garrison it, was ordered to establish road blocks on tracks leading into the town from North and South. Two companies of this unit, according to plan, were placed under command of 7 Inf Bde. By 0900 hrs the leading elements of 1 Armd Bde had reached Jalkot and 17 HORSE was directed to occupy the high ground in the vicinity of Jalkot village, which they did after encountering minor opposition from Hyderabad Forces retreating from Naldrug. In the meantime, infantry of 1 Armd Bde were clearing up the town and capturing the remaining centres of resistance, which were mainly in the fort.

By this time also the Divisional Commander had come up in his jeep to HQ 7 Inf Bde which was established East of Naldrug. Here he had reviewed the situation with his two brigade commanders, had a talk to the prisoners and checked up on the progress of operations. He decided to push Strike Force through as quickly as possible, ordering 1 Armd Bde to keep going behind them with a view to harbouring that night in the Yenagur area and instructed 7 Inf Bde to take over the responsibility for Naldrug village. Instructions were also given them to search all villages on either side of the axis up to a distance of four miles.

By 1045 hrs 1 Armd Bde had cleared the road to enable Strike Force to pass through. Strike Force, which had been moved up to the border immediately on receiving information that the bridge was intact, started to move through Naldrug on to Umerga. By 1515 hrs leading elements of Strike Force had reached Umerga, encountering very little resistance en route. At Umerga itself a certain amount of resistance was encountered from Razakars but this had been quickly cleared up. By the evening Strike Force had established a firm base at Umerga with patrols well East of it.

After Strike Force had gone through, 1 Armd. Bde Gp moved forward behind it into harbour in the Yenagur area, leaving 7 Inf Bde to clear the L of C, mop up in Naldrug and the surrounding villages and wait for their transport.

Operations by Vir Force (9 Inf Bde Gp).

9 Inf Bde had been given the task of capturing Tuljapur with a view to prevent the enemy reinforcing his Naldrug garrison from the North and also to establish 1 MEWAR Inf in Tuljapur. After that they were to move East along the road Tuljapur-Lohara and then South to Yenagur to join the main axis East of Naldrug.

To carry out the above tasks the Brigade commander had split his brigade into two columns. The first column consisting of 2/1 GR supported by one squadron 3 CAV, one battery 9 Para Fd Regt, and a detachment of 10 Fd Coy, was to capture Tuljapur from the North West. The second column consisting of 3 PUNJAB, one troop 18 CAV, one battery 9 Para Fd Regt, and a detachment of 10 Fd Coy, was to move up from Sholapur towards Tuljapur by the main road running North East with the task of capturing the important bridge on the border intact and then attacking Tuljapur from the South. After these two tasks had been completed, the remainder of the brigade was to move up from Sholapur to Tuljapur along the road behind 3 PUNJAB, establish 1 MEWAR Inf at Tuljapur and then move along the axis given in the plan.

Surprisingly, the capture of Tuljapur proved far more difficult than had been anticipated. Tuljapur village itself was situated on a high plateau with difficult approaches. The only access for wheels was from the road Sholapur-Tuljapur and this road was well covered by dug-in positions. The enemy strength was found to consist of one company of regulars and 200 well armed Razakars as well as some Pathans. These defending forces really put up a spirited resistance and as such had to be slowly but systematically liquidated. Four Razakar women had been found fighting side by side with the men and this had caused a little delay. The chivalrous Mewars, true to their Rajput traditions, rounded up these women unarmed before the armed battle started again. However, both the columns described above accomplished their task, though not in the time expected of them; and it was only at 1530 hrs that 1 MEWAR Inf was established in Tuljapur. The Brigade Gp then commenced the advance along the road Tuljapur-Lohara but the leading elements were held up by a nalla in spate within a mile of their starting. It was getting dark which would further delay the advance and hence the Brigade Commander requested permission from Div HQ to harbour in the vicinity of Tuljapur for the night and carry on his advance extremely early the next day. This permission was granted.

Review of Operations on D day.

The Hyderabad Forces had been completely surprised by the two pronged attack on Naldrug and after a first initial resistance lasting about two hours, had either surrendered or started to flee in a most disorganised manner. Our troops advancing, in some cases found bedding rolls still warm from where the defenders had fled, while any warning system that they may have had, had obviously not worked. The placing of the stops along the main road to the East by 7 Inf Bde, had prevented any of the garrison escaping by vehicles. In fact only a few lucky ones, which incidentally included the Garrison Commander, managed to escape and these did so by throwing aside their arms and equipment, disguising themselves as civilians and striking North East across country. The strength of the forces at Naldrug was found to have been the 1 Hyderabad Infantry less one company which had been located at Tuljapur. In addition there were two 25 pr guns, about 300 well armed and equipped Razakars and some 100 Pathans. Casualties among the Hyderabad Army garrison as well as the Razakars and Pathans had been heavy. Roughly 600 of the defenders had been killed and approximately 200 captured. Prisoners included 4 Hyderabad officers and 1 British officer. The former stated that though they had been asked to defend this position to the last man and last round, the spirit of the officers and men were not in the cause at all. They were sure that resistance would stiffen as our troops approached Hyderabad but expressed themselves ignorant of the plans of the Hyderabad Army. This ignorance was very clearly not put on, as the prisoners were only too anxious to give information. The facts appeared to be that they did not know because they had not been told anything by their higher command. The officer-prisoners stated however that the Naldrug position had been expected and designed to delay any Indian Union advance from between 24 hours to three days.

The British officer captured was a Lieut T. T. Moore, an ex-British Army Commando and Special Service Officer, who had taken service with the Hyderabad Army after August 1947. He had been captured by one of the 2 R SIKH road blocks East of Naldrug at about 0830 hrs, while driving in a loaded Jeep, extremely fast, in the direction of Naldrug. On first capture, he stated that under instructions from his High Commissioner he had resigned from the Hyderabad Army and was leaving the State as quickly as he could. On further questioning, interrogation and search however, it was discovered that his Jeep was full of demolition explosives, while personal papers, which included letters of identification to Hyderabad Army units, indicated that this officer was to be responsible for arranging demolitions. He had been sent out at top speed by Hyderabad Army HQ to demolish the Naldrug

NALDRUG

A destroyed Hyderabad 25 pr.

and other bridges. He had apparently been told the night before that the Indian Union advance would take place on 15 Sep. There is no doubt, that had D day been put off till 15 Sep, surprise would have been lost and considerable delay may have been encountered. Lieut Moore was handed over to Sholapur (Indep) Sub-Area for despatch to Southern Command.

On further interrogation, officers of the Hyderabad Army taken at Naldrug stated, that a section of two 25 pr guns had been allocated to operate in the area. Originally both had been located near Jalkot but later one had been moved forward into Naldrug itself. This was the gun that had shelled 1 Armd Bde advance. Both guns were captured in good condition by the Indian Union forces in the first hour of the advance.

Location as at 1800 *hrs on D day.* (See Map A).

Despite the "fog of war" which had descended during the first three hours of the advance, a 'fog' which is encountered so often during the very beginning of any battle, operations had gone very well. By 1800 hrs Strike Force had penetrated about 28 miles and had seized and made a strong base at Umerga with patrols Eastwards. 1 Armd Bde Gp had moved up and concentrated in the Yenagur area together with all their transport, thus being immediately behind Strike Force and also ready for an immediate move. 7 Inf Bde Gp was astride the road between Naldrug-Jalkot, in complete possession of these two areas and searching villages four miles to either side. 9 Inf Bde Gp on the other hand, had not had so much success. Owing to delay in completing their operations plus bad roads and tracks, their advance had been stopped and they were harboured 4 miles South East of Tuljapur on the road Tuljapur-Naldrug. Main Div HQ owing to lack of road space and thus according to plan had not moved forward on this day and was located on the border. Rear Div HQ was still concentrated in Sholapur. The locations of formations are shown in map Q. Orders for the next day's operations had been issued and the Staff was busy confirming them.

Administration.

Administratively too the situation was excellent. By nightfall the brigaded B echelons had reached their parent formations. Stomachs and petrol tanks were full while the ammunition expended during the day had been replenished. 2nd line tpt was full and ready to move to replenish B echelons the next morning. Personnel casualties, both our own and the enemy had been treated and evacuated, prisoners were safely in the PW camp while the dead had been buried. There had been no A or B vehicle casualties, the latter a surprising but a pleasing feature in view of the number of vehicles involved. Though something of a refugee problem had been anticipated, it was remarkable that no refugees of any kind had been encountered. Troops searching villages had been ordered not to upset the village administration and to treat all communities fairly. This in itself was restoring confidence to a great degree in the civilian population.

Our casualties had been

    Killed .. .. 7 (incl one JCO),
    Wounded .. .. 9 (of which one died later).
    Prisoners of war .. Nil.

The enemy casualties had been

    Killed .. .. About 632 (incl 2 officers and 4 JCOs).
    Wounded .. .. 14.
    Captured .. .. 200 (incl 4 officers and 1 JCO).

On the whole the first day of operations had gone according to plan and been a complete success.

CHAPTER VII

D Plus 1 Day—14 Sep, 48

The general plan for D plus 1 day was to continue the eastward advance along the main road as rapidly as possible with the object of trying to capture the line running North and South of Rajasur about 30 miles further on. This would give our forces control over the important cross roads 6 miles West of Homnabad. This would also poise them for the attack on Homnabad the next day and also block roads leading into this town. Orders had been issued for an advance with Strike Force in the lead and 1 Armd Bde following in close support. 9 Inf Bde was to move through 7 Inf Bde and follow up behind 1 Armd Bde. 7 Inf Bde was to remain static in the clearing up task that had been allotted to them previously and were also to rest and wait for their transport. Rear Div HQ was to move to its next firm base from Sholapur to Naldrug.

A careful study of the map and an inspection of aerial photographs, combined with information that had been obtained about possible defensive plans, seemed to suggest that the Hyderabad Army would probably hold a strong defensive position in the area two miles East and West of the village of Talmud. The ground here was hilly with very soft going in the valleys. There appeared to be a number of good observation posts and suitable gun positions covering the main line of advance, while the position as such was difficult to outflank. For four miles the road ran through a narrow defile and at the end of this defile there was a sudden steep climb on to the Bidar plateau. In fact, by any standards, it was ground ideally suited to a defensive position particularly against armour. Aerial reconnaissance had shown considerable defensive preparations as having been made and consequently a certain amount of anxiety was felt about the delaying powers of this feature.

Instructions given to Strike Force were necessarily detailed and it was to reconnoitre thoroughly the Talmud position. If the opposition intended to give battle there, Strike Force was to try and capture a few observation posts as quickly as possible at the same time denying the Hyderabad Army any observation, while the remainder of the Division was forming up for the attack. Naturally they also had to find the flanks, get information from all sources as to possible opposition strengths and in fact do the normal advanced guard tasks.

It had rained heavily during the night, for the first and only time during the operations, and the roads, nallas and tracks were extremely difficult to negotiate. Bridge classifications were uncertain and delay was to be expected if the tanks were to make detours.

SEQUENCE OF OPERATIONS.

Operations by Strike Force.

At 0615 hrs Strike Force resumed the advance. In view of the possible difficulties of the Talmud position as well as the slippery road surface, the advance was slow and troops of Strike Force moved fairly cautiously searching the adjoining close country thoroughly and taking no chances. It was exasperating but it was necessary. Just then there was a stroke of luck, one of those gifts that the Gods of Battle sometimes hand one. Quite by chance at about 0800 hrs the Divisional Commander, tired of listening to reports of slow movement from his leading troops, tuned in to the Hyderabad Radio News in English. Imagine his surprise to find the dulcet tones of a woman announcer, stating that though Hyderabad troops had gallantly defended the Talmud position, it had been captured by the enemy who were advancing. While this announcement was being made our leading troops were still one mile from Talmud.

This information changed the whole situation. With a shout of joy the Divisional Commander immediately called up the Strike Force Commander, Lt Col Ram Singh. Much to the latter's surprise he was ordered to advance as quickly as possible without searching the area at all. Rather incredulously he asked the reason for this change of orders and when these were given him, Strike Force started to move forward extremely quickly in their normal advanced guard role. The bound for the day Rajasur, was reached by 1230 hrs, without any opposition except some sniping. Once there, Strike Force started to search the village and form a firm base. By 1430 hrs the town had been found clear except for a few Razakars, while road blocks had been established on the East of the town to prevent any persons carrying information to Homnabad and subsequently Hyderabad. Troops had also blocked all crossroads leading into Rajasur and so into Homnabad. Div Tac HQ was up at Rajasur by 1300 hrs and together with Lt Col Ram Singh and Brig Verma, the latter who had been collected en route, plans were discussed for the next day's operations.

The abandonment of the Talmud defile had been an extraordinary and inexplicable piece of luck. As described before, the position was a strong one. It was well dug-in and was found to be stocked with both food and ammunition. A determined force of battalion strength could have delayed the advance for 24 hrs certainly, if not, longer. Later it was discovered that the rapid advance on the first day plus an air strike on the position by a flight of Tempest aircraft also on the first day, had upset the defenders morale. They had abandoned their positions as soon as possible and fallen back.

Operations by Smash Force (1 Armd Bde Gp).

Also starting at 0615 hrs in the morning, 1 Armd Bde followed up Strike Force ready to support them should they need such support. This support was not required. During the advance, working on a system of pickets, they did a certain amount of searching of the villages up to 3 miles on either side of the road. This, while slowing up their move, made for security. Their orders were to harbour just West of Rajasur.

When Div Tac HQ, which had moved off early to be behind Strike Force during the advance, arrived in Umerga they found a curious state of affairs in this large village. The night before Lt Col Ram Singh had reported the attitude of the inhabitants both Hindu and Muslim, as having been sullen and non-co-operative. Apparently it was the HQ of a big Jagirdari and as such, the administration was different from that pertaining in the rest of the State with inferior officials, most of whom were not declaring themselves. When Div Tac HQ arrived they found 1 Armd Bde Tac HQ already there and dealing with an attempt on the part of both communities to loot each other. The Commanders, with their small Tac HQ immediately took charge of the situation and the looting was stopped forthwith. All inhabitants then were gathered together, given a homily on the subject of communal peace and told that the Indian Union Army had come into the State to maintain law and order and to punish all law-breakers irrespective of the community to which they belonged. As the officials could not be found, local officials were appointed and a detachment from the first infantry unit coming up was put on once again to searching the town. This searching proved to be a long and difficult process and even uptil the morning of the next day, groups of Razakars and Arabs who had taken shelter in the outlying houses and fields kept up a steady sniping of personnel either in or passing through the village. This sniping fortunately caused no casualties but was irritating, to say the least of it.

As 1 Armd Bde was coming into harbour about 1430 hrs, a report was received of a large concentration of Razakars in position at the village of Kalyani 6 miles North of the main road. These Razakars, well armed, had apparently taken charge of the village and were determined to fight it out. Anxious to end this nuisance quickly, one squadron of 3 CAV and a company of 4 GWALIOR Inf was immediately detached, firstly to contain these Razakars and prevent them from interfering with the rest of the advance and secondly to liquidate them. A four hour action ensued against this irregular armed force estimated at about 500. As a result of this operation, about 100 Razakars were killed, about 200 were captured, and a large assortment of arms and ammunition were taken. On our side, the CO of 4 GWALIOR Inf was seriously wounded, while his unit suffered two other casualties. This rapid and successful action cleared up a possible threat to the L of C and also had an extraordinarily good effect as far as further Razakar resistance was concerned.

Operations by Vir Force (9 Inf Bde Gp).

9 Inf Bde found that the original route that had been given them, that is, via Lohara-Yenagur was impassable owing to the bad going. This information had been passed very early in the morning to Divisional HQ. The Divisional Commander had then ordered that they should move down the main track from Tuljapur to Naldrug, pass through 7 Inf Bde and move up behind 1 Armd Bde. To ensure the safety of the L of C, they were given the tasks of patrolling up to 4 miles on either side of the road, investigating the larger villages and mopping up if necessary. During the day instructions were sent to them to harbour on the Rajasur plateau, West of 1 Armd Bde. 9 Inf Bde had no difficulty in executing these orders.

Operations by Kill Force (7 Inf Bde Gp).

7 Inf Bde whose transport had still not reached them owing to the heavy rain and the impassability of track, was ordered to continue with the task that had been given to them the day before, that is, the searching of the country between Naldrug and Yenagur. They were also told to rest as much as possible, get up their transport that day and be ready for a long and early move the next morning. In the execution of this task very little opposition was met.

Moves of HQ, 1 Armd Div.

In the movement plan for the day, the moves of Main and Rear Div HQ had to be fitted in. Main Div HQ moved to Umerga and Rear Div HQ moved to Naldrug. To Sholapur (Indep) Sub-Area was handed over the responsibility for that portion of the road from Sholapur to Naldrug and two companies of 4 GWALIOR Inf which had been left at Naldrug reverted to command of Sholapur (Indep) Sub-Area.

Administration.

By 1500 hrs all HQ had reached their harbour positions for the night. Admittedly there were few troops in the harbour at that time and those that were there were mostly administrative details. The others were all busy employed on searches, the establishment of road blocks, the improvement of roads, the clearing of all threats from the L of C and the myriad other tasks that troops have to do when not fighting an actual battle. Second line transport had moved up in the morning and refilled all B echelons, which had then moved forward to their respective harbour areas. Once again by the evening of D plus 1 day, all echelons had been refilled and second line transport was returning to its base to stock up again. Except for the CO of 4 GWALIOR Inf getting wounded at Kalyani and two other casualties, no other losses had been incurred among our own troops and the 250 odd Razakar casualties and prisoners, particularly from the village of Kalyani were awaiting evacuation. There had been no A vehicle casualties while the B vehicle casualties were three. By nightfall, once again, the situation seemed to be right, even according to the book.

Review of Operations on D plus 1 day.

Despite the heavy rain and consequent difficult going, the advance had proceeded very favourably. The opposition encountered had been negligible and the surprising abandonment of the well prepared positions in the Talmud defile, had helped operations considerably. Once again no refugees had been encountered. Troops had to take certain action in regard to the civilian population to prevent the looting of an occasional house or shop. Looting was prevented with a firm hand and this had an extremely good effect in restoring confidence, particularly among the minority community and indicating to the majority community that the Indian Army was most impartial in any action that it took. It was apparent however, that the Civil Administration Teams which were to function in the wake of the troops were required up at Divisional HQ as soon as possible. This need was mentioned to Southern Command and it was agreed in the first instance to send up the team for Bidar, which was the next district to be entered on D plus 2 day. Southern Command also agreed to send up the teams for Osmanabad district on their own. The troops were in excellent form. It was only too apparent that after the first hard knock, the Hyderabad Army was moving back as fast as possible. Though their future plans were not known, it was thought that they would possibly hold the Zahirabad-Bidar line in strength and would certainly hold a really strong position around Hyderabad City itself.

Location as at 1800 hrs on D plus 1 day. (See Map R).

CHAPTER VIII.

D Plus 2 Day—15 Sep, 48.

The reader will remember that though the Hyderabad forces plan was not known in detail, it was always thought they would make a stand on the line Zahirabad-Bidar. To make a long bound on D plus 2 day therefore would have been folly as it would mean reaching a well defended area, late in the afternoon with petrol tanks empty and tired troops. Also any plan for the advance this day had to consider two more factors. Firstly, the occupation and clearance of Homnabad town and secondly, the beginnings of a two pronged drive to clear Bidar airstrip. One of the subsidiary tasks that had been given to 1 Armd Div by HQ Southern Command had been the capture and clearance of Bidar airfield, so as to allow our Air Forces to have a closer base for the final assault on Hyderabad should it become necessary. The attack on Bidar had originally been planned as a two pronged move. A force was to be detached at Homnabad to move North-East up the secondary road direct to Bidar, while the main thrust was to capture the cross-roads at Zahirabad and then detach a force to move northwards along the main road to Bidar. This method of advance would also trap the Bidar garrison if they were to try to escape into Hyderabad City.

Working with these objects in view, the plan of operations for D plus 2 day was generally speaking a limited one. The first objective was to surround the town of Homnabad with Strike Force and let 1 Armd Bde Group clear it with their infantry. While this was going on, Strike Force was to move forward to lightly reconnoitre the Zahirabad cross-roads. After their search, 1 Armd Bde Group was to swing North-East and move a little way along the track Homnabad-Bidar while 9 Inf Bde Group was to take on a second search of Homnabad town. 7 Inf Bde Group was to move up and take over the area Rajasur-Homnabad from 9 Inf Bde Group and continue the search of all villages 4 miles on either side of the road, with the object of keeping the L of C clear.

Sequence of Operations.

Operations by Strike Force and Smash Force.

By 0615 hrs Strike Force had moved forward and picketed the outskirts of Homnabad town and by 0800 hrs 1 Armd Bde Group was well engaged in the search. The arrival of our troops was a complete surprise to the citizens of Homnabad. They had been listening to Hyderabad Radio and not to the AIR. As a result they were under the impression that the Indian advance was held up and the Hyderabad Army Forces who had moved back from Talmud, had gone through the town at night in small groups, unseen and unheard by the mass of the people. The few townspeople who had seen the withdrawing troops had been told that all was going well. The extent of the surprise can be shown by the fact that at about 0730 hrs in the morning, a car containing a Hyderabadi official from the districts, complete with his whole family including a grandmother and grandchildren, drove straight into the Travellers' Bungalow just on the West of the town from the North. As Tac HQ 1 Armd Bde and later Tac Div HQ was established there, they were extremely surprised and perhaps a little frightened to see Indian Union troops well in possession and going methodically about their duties. This surprise was however tempered by another kind of surprise, when they found nothing but courtesy and kindness shown them. Brig Verma made personal arrangements for their safe custody, food and drink and later when the Divisional Commander came up, arrangements were made to send them back to the place from which they had come, with a military escort to see no trouble occurred. This incident received considerable publicity in the Press later and did much to make the Muslim officials feel that the Indian Army were not the uncouth ogres that Hyderabadi propaganda had made them out to be.

In Homnabad itself there was a little sporadic resistance from Arab treasury guards and a few Razakars. These elements were very quickly isolated and rounded up, while a search for arms as well as their voluntary surrender produced large quantities of lethal weapons. The town officials, both Hindu and Muslim after their first fear was overcome, co-operated well with the troops. They stated that in Homnabad itself there had never been much communal trouble and this was found to be correct as the situation in the town quietened down extremely quickly. Orders were passed that the town was to remain under control of the local officers and to be out of bounds to troops. Let it be quite clear that this order was not given because of what the troops would do, but to try and restore confidence among the local officials. This it succeeded in doing admirably.

Immediately the search of Homnabad had been taken over by 1 Armd Bde, Strike Force resumed the advance towards Zahirabad. The first opposition troops encountered were about 7 miles East of Homnabad when 2 lorry loads of Hyderabad Forces, strangely enough moving West were ambushed. Unfortunately for these troops, they ran into our leading tanks. Both vehicles were destroyed immediately by gunfire, while of the personnel 24 were killed and 13 taken prisoner. Once again complete surprise was achieved as questioning of prisoners showed that they had no idea as to how fast we had moved forward. Hyderabad Radio after conceding Talmud had not let us advance any further.

After completing the first search of Homnabad, 1 Armd Bde started to move along the direct road to Bidar. After going 4 miles, the leading elements reported that the so-called road was only a track and this track was quite unusable owing to bad going, no bridges over the nullas and the fords in spate. These spates were of course, the result of the heavy monsoon rains which had been falling just before the Police Action started.

This report from 1 Armd Bde placed the Division in rather a quandary, as it meant that the original plan of a two pronged attack was completely knocked on the head. The advance to Zahirabad would have to continue on a single axis and if the position was held it would have to be taken frontally. Bidar would have to be taken from the South, after the capture of Zahirabad, while at the same time the advance to Hyderabad would have to go forward. This would mean a regrouping of forces particularly the artillery and engineer support now necessary and this regrouping would take time.

Locations on D plus 2 day. (See Map R).

Bearing this future regrouping in mind and also realising that it was pointless to get an unbalanced force to Zahirabad in the late afternoon, combined with a wish to rest the troops and transport, all of which had had three long and hard days, particularly the drivers of the maintenance lorries, the Divisional Commander issued the following brief orders. 1 Armd Bde Group was to harbour just North-West of Homnabad. Strike Force was not to advance further than 10 miles East of Homnabad. Main Div HQ was to move up immediately as far forward as possible, in fact, just behind Strike Force, so as to be well positioned for controlling the operations and regrouping the next day. 7 Inf Bde Group was to harbour just West of Homnabad and be responsible for guarding all roads coming on to the L of C, while 9 Inf Bde Group was to move forward to an area just South West of Main Div HQ. This move of 9 Inf Bde had two objects. Firstly, the positioning of infantry well forward in case they were needed the next day and also suitable protection for Main Div HQ in the event of any trouble.

Review of operations on D plus 2 day.

Though operations had started off by going according to plan, the discovery that the track Homnabad-Bidar was completely unusable, had necessitated a major change in plan. The results of the speed of advance were becoming more and more apparent and it was obvious that Hyderabad Army HQ had no idea how far the Indian troops had penetrated. The Hyderabad Army for the second day had not been seen except in small packets, while a few Razakars and Arabs had held out but possibly more through fear of what might happen to them if captured, rather than any deep-seated conviction to fight to the last. The morale of the opposition was rapidly cracking.

As a result of the previous two days experience in clearing villages, on D plus 2 day new tactics had been adopted. Troops engaged in clearing operations stood well back from the village and sent some locals, whom they had caught in the fields, into the village concerned with an assurance to every one there, whether Hindu or Muslim, that if they came out and handed in their arms, no further action would be taken against them. This new method was extremely successful, as once the arms were handed in, the villagers were left alone with a few well chosen words on the advantages of communal amity. As has been stated many times before in these pages, the object of 1 Armd Div was to reach Hyderabad as quickly as possible with as little interference to the local population as possible and to try and establish among all whom they met, the Indian Government's policy of a secular state.

In this review of operations on D plus 2 day, Strike Force and 1 Armd Bde seem to figure more prominently than the two infantry brigade groups. This is only because their operations were perhaps more spectacular than those of the infantry. Let it be quite clear, however, it was only because the Hyderabad Army were not standing to give battle, that the infantry brigade groups were not being employed in the direct attacking role, as they had been on the first day. It should also be quite clear that no rapid advance could have been made, had not the two infantry brigades put in such thorough and solid work, in consolidating positions taken, in clearing dangers to the L of C and in fact successfully accomplishing those seemingly secondary but nevertheless dangerous and arduous tasks, which are so necessary in a successful battle.

Administration.

By this time the L of C was getting a little on the long side, the turn round being in the nature of 120 miles. Hence the days limited advance had also not been dictated entirely by operational considerations but also from a survey of the administrative situation. It was essential that the supply dumps moving forward behind 1 Armd Div got the opportunity to move before the next day's operations. Such a move could only be accomplished, if the 1 Armd Div move was a short one. Once again however, by 1800 hrs, all casualties had been evacuated, all dead cremated or buried, all B echelons had rejoined their groups for the night, while the new plan was being worked out in conjunction with the Brigade Commanders and senior staff officers. Administratively one of the most remarkable thing was the lack of vehicle casualties. The CIEME, responsible for the recovery and repair of vehicles, was in fact heard to protest that just to keep his units occupied, he had been repairing the few Hyderabadi vehicles that had been captured and putting them back on the road. The CRIE was also another disappointed man. His bridging train, which had been formed to deal quickly with any demolition, had not been tested out. He was heard to say that he would have to start demolitions himself. Apart from these two however, every one was in very high spirits.

In these rather scrappy operations, unfortunately the casualties had been a little high. Hyderabad casualties were:—

Irregulars.
  Killed 200
  Captured 66

Hyderabad Army.
  Killed 24
  Captured 13

Our own casualties were:—

  Killed JCOs .. 1   These killed and wounded were
     OR   .. 10   largely the result of sniping by
  Wounded JCOs .. 3   the Irregular Forces in the mop-
     OR   .. 29   ping up of villages.

CHAPTER IX.

D Plus 3 Day—16 Sep, 48.

It will be remembered that on D plus 3 day, opposition was expected on the line Zahirabad-Bidar. Also, as Bidar could not be taken from two directions, a frontal attack from the South would be necessary. At the same time, it was obvious that while Bidar was being captured and consolidated, no slowing up could be allowed of the present excellent rate of advance, as such slowing up might give the Hyderabad Army the breathing space to reform.

Information about the enemy had been received that at Zahirabad there was a minimum of two companies from 3 HS Inf and possibly the whole battalion itself, while in Bidar the strength of the garrison was not known but it was thought to be a company but a company possibly reinforced by elements that had retreated from the western front. What irregular forces might be met was not known, but Hyderabad Radio had been putting out stories of " gallant " Razakars being rushed to the western front. From a talk with the prisoners who had been captured on the evening of D plus 2 day, it was apparent that a certain number of mines had been laid on the main road but the location of these mines was not known. It was also obviously necessary to regroup, this regrouping being necessitated by the major change in plan.

The completed plan for D plus 3 day was, therefore, for Strike Force to go forward initially and capture the crossroads slightly West of Zahirabad. Once having established themselves here, they were to halt and allow 1 Armd Bde to take the lead on the main axis, through Zahirabad eastwards. Strike Force was then to swing northwards and make for Bidar. In this new role, it was felt that 1 Armd Bde had to have under command another battalion of infantry and for this purpose 2/1 GR was detached from 9 Inf Bde Group and placed under command of 1 Armd Bde; while to strengthen the armour, a squadron of 3 CAV which had been operating with 9 Inf Bde also came back under command of its own unit. It was further ordered that once the Zahirabad crossroads had been captured, when 1 Armd Bde was passing through, the battery of medium guns originally grouped with Strike Force would leave them and come under command of 1 Armd Bde. There was certainly no need for medium guns at Bidar while it was essential that these guns were well forward in the main advance. At Div HQ it was felt that this day's operations would be crucial. Once the Zahirabad-

"OPERATION POLO"

Bidar line was captured and Bidar airfield secured, any heavy resistance outside Hyderabad City itself could easily be dealt with, as close and direct air support would become available.

SEQUENCE OF OPERATIONS.

Operations by Strike Force.

At 0615 hrs Strike Force resumed the advance but met their first check an hour later at a partially demolished masonry bridge about 4 miles East of their harbour area. A quick search was carried out and the bridge was found to be mined. Fortunately some of these mines had been set off unwittingly by two bullocks who had strolled across the bridge in the very early hours of the morning. The ensuing explosions had been responsible for the partial demolition. Work was started on clearing the mines and making a diversion over the nalla. At 0800 hrs the diversion had been completed and the advance continued but a little more slowly. While the diversion was being reconnoitred and the mines were being cleared, a hurried engineer reconnaissance of the bridge was made and for the first time since the start of operations, the bridging train came into use. Within 1½ hours of the reconnaissance being completed, a 30 ft class 40 Bailey bridge had been built and was carrying all vehicles of the advancing troops.

The advance of Strike Force was somehow slower than usual. This was possibly brought about by the armoured element, who having met mines for the first time, were perhaps unduly cautious in their speed of advance. A swift admonition to the CO, who was told that the Div Recce Regt was not really doing its job unless it was losing one tank a day on mines or by gunfire, produced good effects and the advance started to go a little faster. By 1215 hrs Strike Force had reached the road junction just West of Zahirabad and encountered hostile enemy fire. Here again the tanks of Strike Force, while showing initiative, neglected to remember the orders that had been given to them, which was not to proceed beyond the outskirts of Zahirabad. In their enthusiasm, they advanced into the town itself and started to clear up the opposition, a task they should have left to the tanks of 1 Armd Bde. Therefore delay occurred once more, while the tanks of Strike Force were extricated from Zahirabad and the tanks of 1 Armd Bde took over. Once this had been done however, Strike Force continued on its proper role, the advance northwards to Bidar.

Operations by Smash Force (1 Armd Bde Group).

The clearing of Zahirabad was a very slow process. It appeared to be well defended mainly by irregulars, while thick woods around

OUTSIDE ZAHIRABAD

(from L to R) Brig Verma Comd 1 Armd Bde, Maj Gen J. N. Chaudhuri; Brig Litchfield, C Arty 1 Armd Div.

the town and the close grouping of the houses made it essential that the clearance was extremely thorough. Divisional orders had always been that minimum force should be used, as it was not the intention of the Indian Union troops to do more damage or destruction than was absolutely essential to achieve the object. 1 Armd Bde Commander, Brig Verma, finding his advance getting held up, asked permission once again to use his 75 mm guns. The last time permission to use these guns had been given was at Naldrug. Permission was granted for a minimum number of rounds to be fired and once the 75s had come into action and fired a total of 12 rounds, opposition cleared up fairly quickly. A battalion from 9 Inf Bde, 1 BIHAR, was moved forward just behind 1 Armd Bde to take over the task of searching Zahirabad town a second time, while 1 Armd. Bde moved on. The constant delays on D plus 3 day had exasperated both the Divisional Commander and the Brigade Commanders to a great degree and once Zahirabad was cleared, 1 Armd Bde moved forward extremely well and fast.

The opposition after withdrawing from Zahirabad town had taken up a defensive position on the high ground East of the town where they offered a certain amount of resistance. This position was immediately isolated by the 2/1 GR, who were detached and put into action against this resistance which they cleared up by nightfall.

Meanwhile Strike Force's advance along the road Zahirabad-Bidar had been fairly slow. Hyderabadi troops retreating from Bidar had been encountered at Malkapur and engaged. This action took a certain amount of time and though Strike Force followed up extremely quickly, trying to reach Bidar that night, owing to the failing light however, they had to harbour 4 miles South of Bidar that day.

Both 7 Inf Bde and 9 Inf Bde Groups were actively employed throughout the day, in patrolling and clearing the villages on either side of the main axis. A certain amount of opposition was initially encountered from Razakars but on vigorous action being taken, these irregulars fled.

At about 1515 hrs the Divisional Commander with his Tac HQ was right up with the leading tanks of 1 Armd Bde chatting to Brig Verma, when he was suddenly passed a message from his Main Div HQ that an enemy aircraft had fired two rockets and machine-gunned Main Div HQ. The casualties reported were 3 OR wounded and one Jeep set on fire. This was the first report of the use of airpower by the enemy and the Divisional Commander was extremely dubious about it being an enemy aircraft. He thought perhaps that one of our own supporting aircraft had mistaken its target and attacked Main Div HQ, possibly thinking it to be Bidar. However the only thing to do was to go back and check up. On his return to Main Div, he found considerable discussion going on as to the identity of the aircraft which had attacked our own troops. Argument was fast and furious and the exponents of both schools were about equally divided. Determined to clear up the matter as soon as possible, the Divisional Commander immediately called up Southern Command on the RT rear link, asked for the senior Air Officer Commanding and flatly accused him of allowing one of his own aircraft to attack Main Div HQ. He was gratified to find that this was actually what had happened. The young pilot of the aircraft concerned, had lost his way and rocketed Main Div HQ, thinking it to be an enemy concentration at Bidar. The mistake had been discovered while he was being de-briefed at Poona and apparently the young man had received no mean 'rocket' himself. Fortunately not much harm had been done by the incident and in fact a certain amount of good may have been done. The troops had certainly become more air conscious, slit trenches and camouflage improved themselves in the twinkling of an eye.

Locations as at 1800 *hrs on D plus* 3 *day* (See Map S).

1 Armd Bde boldly led by Brig Verma, had done a first-class job in the clearing of Zahirabad and getting forward as fast as possible.

At 1800 hrs on D plus 3 day 16 September the locations of the various columns were as follows:—

  Strike Force .. .. 4 Miles South of Bidar airfield.
  1 Armd Bde Group .. 8 „ East of Zahirabad.

  One battalion 9 Inf Group (1 BIHAR) in Zahirabad.

  Main Div HQ and 9 Inf Bde Group, at their original location.

  7 Inf Bde Group .. .. Still clearing up around the area of Homnabad and forward to Main Div HQ.

  Rear Div HQ at Rajasur.

Administration.

With the original delays that had taken place in the morning, road space had been taken up and so it had not been possible to move up the B echelon of 1 Armd Bde to join its parent group by nightfall. It was not considered safe for this B echelon to move up at night and orders were given for it to join up immediately after first light the next morning. The delay that would occur in starting off the next day, owing to replenishment having to take place, had to be accepted.

Otherwise from the administrative side, the situation was normal. The delays had allowed the 3rd line dumps to move forward and this was an advantage for the Divisional maintenance columns. For the first time since the beginning of operations, the Divisional 2nd line transport managed to get a short turn round and consequently a much deserved rest before replenishing the next morning.

Review of Operations—D plus 3 day.

The speed of operations this day had been comparatively slow in the beginning owing to the partially damaged bridge met early on and to the sporadic but stiff resistance offered in the vicinity of Zahirabad. Delay had also been caused by the armoured element of Strike Force, moving forward too slowly at the start and later getting involved with opposition forces in Zahirabad. Strike Force's northward advance had been halted by failing light and the surprise appearance of Hyderabad troops at Malkapur; though perhaps the Hyderabadis were more surprised than our own troops. The Hyderabad Forces were still uncertain of where our columns were and they always thought we were moving slower than in fact we actually were.

Advantage had been taken this day to move Rear HQ close up behind the Division; and Sholapur Indep Sub-Area also took the opportunity to move up their supply dumps which had been on wheels at Umerga into Rajasur. This meant that the turn round of 2nd line transport was considerably reduced while the protection of the L of C behind Rajasur became the task of Sholapur Indep Sub-Area and not of the Division, who thus had the task of looking only forward for the final phase.

Mention has been made earlier on, of the value of the divisional intercept service formed from 1 Armd Div Signal Regt and located at Main Div HQ. By this time all messages being sent out by the Hyderabad Army Commander were being picked up at Div HQ and were probably reaching 1 Armd Div Commander before they reached the Hyderabad Army Commanders to whom they were addressed. The tones of such intercepted messages as the operations went on, were very interesting to note. At the beginning they had been mainly tactical with the usual exhortations about justice being on Hyderabad's side. By D plus 3 day, the tone of the message had changed and all orders seemed to be extremely muddled and on a 'sauve-qui-peut' basis. Also the name of the Almighty started creeping in very frequently. It is an old adage in the Army that should any Commander start sending messages asking for the Almighty to be either under command or in support, the end as far as he is concerned is rapidly approaching. This trend was most heartening. The replies back from the Hyderabad field commanders were even more curious. Orders or no orders they were obviously going back fast, while to save their reputations they were reporting battles that had never occurred. These false reports must have added to the confusion at Hyderabad Army HQ.

That evening the Divisional Commander and the Army Commander had a long discussion on the RT link to Poona. The day's progress and trend of intercepted messages was discussed. The Army Commander felt certain that the Hyderabad Army had no intention of continuing the fight and were preparing to surrender. With this the Divisional Commander agreed. The Army Commander said that he would broadcast a surrender message to Major-General Syed Ahmed. El-Edroos the next day and the results of such message would be passed to the Armd Div as quickly as possible.

Within the Division itself there was a lot of speculation as to what the next move by the Hyderabad State Forces would be. The Divisional Commander however, was quite certain that a surrender was bound to come, either the next day or the day after. This certainly had been further reinforced by the result of a careful study of the intercepted messages as well as the interrogation of any prisoners captured. There was no news of a massacre of the Hindu population by the Razakars, in fact the Razakars had disappeared like snow before a hot wind. However, speed and more speed to reach Hyderabad City quickly was essential. The presence of Indian troops at the capital itself could be the only certain safeguard against trickery and massacre.

CHAPTER X.

D Plus 4 Day—17 Sep, 48.

As will be seen from the events of the last Chapter, much was expected on D plus 4 day. Though the majority of the Division were not quite certain as to whether the Hyderabad Army would surrender on this day or not, it was absolutely certain however, that Bidar airfield would be captured and that the Division would reach within medium gun range of Hyderabad City by nightfall. Certainly, the day would produce some form of excitement.

The plan for D plus 4 day was fairly simple, just a continuation of the plans that had been made for D plus 3 day; Strike Force was to resume its interrupted advance on Bidar and secure the airfield as soon as possible. Once the airfield was secured their engineer detachment was to get the field in working order, so that by that afternoon at the latest, Dakotas could land there. 1 Armd Bde Group with 2/1 GR still under command was to advance along the main road Zahirabad-Hyderabad and capture Sadaseopet and then keep on going. 7 Inf Bde Group was to move through 9 Inf Bde Group to Digwar, a village commanding an important crossroad East of Zahirabad, and to hold and search it. 9 Inf Bde Group was to take over Zahirabad and also to search various important villages along the main axis of advance. Main Div HQ was to move to the Zahirabad crossroads and Rear Div HQ was to move to the area vacated by Main Div HQ. The L of C up as far as Homnabad was to be handed over to Sholapur Indep Sub-Area, who were also to move 3rd line supplies as far forward as possible. (See Map S).

Sequence of Operations.

Operations by Smash Force (1 Armd Bde Group).

Owing to the fact that the Armd. Bde B echelon had not joined the main body the evening before, the start was somewhat delayed to allow for replenishment, particularly that of fuel for the tanks. While this was being done, so as not to waste time, a squadron of 3 CAV was sent out at first light for a reconnaissance down the road, forward of 1 Armd Bde, with instructions to seize as a first bound the high ground East of milestone 54. Approximately 2 miles East of the harbour, while passing through a defile, the leading tank of this squadron ran over a mine and blew off one of its tracks. This was the first time that a properly laid out minefield had been encountered and there was some little delay in clearing it, particularly as the approaches had been booby-trapped. Fortunately, however, the defile and the minefield had not been covered by fire and consequently clearance did not necessitate an action. On investigation it was found that the mine that had blown off the track of the leading 3 CAV tank, had been electrically exploded by a demolition party covering the minefield. Immediately after igniting that one mine however, the enemy demolition party had fled.

The advance of 1 Armd. Bde Group continued but on account of the nature of the ground on either side of the road, a very small degree of search was possible. However, by this time the conviction that the enemy would not hold at all, was appearing to be correct and even at the risk of being ambushed, 1 Armd Bde Group was ordered to advance on a very narrow front indeed, sacrificing security for speed and distance gained. By 1200 hrs the town of Sadaseopet was reached without opposition. A large gathering of local inhabitants welcomed the advent of the Indian Union troops and this was the first time that such scenes of enthusiasm, which were to become a commonplace later, were first met. Local reports gave no indication of possible enemy action but suggested that small parties of enemy troops were in the area. Clearing Sadaseopet, 1 Armd Bde Group advanced another 6 miles and on instructions from Div HQ harboured early, by 1400 hrs, so as to enable complete maintenance to be done to all vehicles, particularly tanks, to prepare for what was expected to be a final assault the next morning.

Operations by Kill Force (7 Inf Bde Group) and Vir Force (9 Inf Bde Group).

9 Inf Bde Group and 7 Inf Bde Group also moved up to complete their tasks and found no opposition in the searches that they had to do, either from the regulars or irregulars. In fact, large numbers of the majority community were met, who welcomed troops with enthusiasm and said that there were neither Hyderabad Army troops nor Razakars in the vicinity. Main Div HQ moved early and established itself on the Zahirabad crossroads.

Operations by Strike Force.

While this movement was going on, Strike Force made a rapid advance securing Bidar airfield by 1000 hrs. No opposition of any sort was encountered by them. The inhabitants of Bidar stated that the troops that had been defending the airfield, had fled the evening before

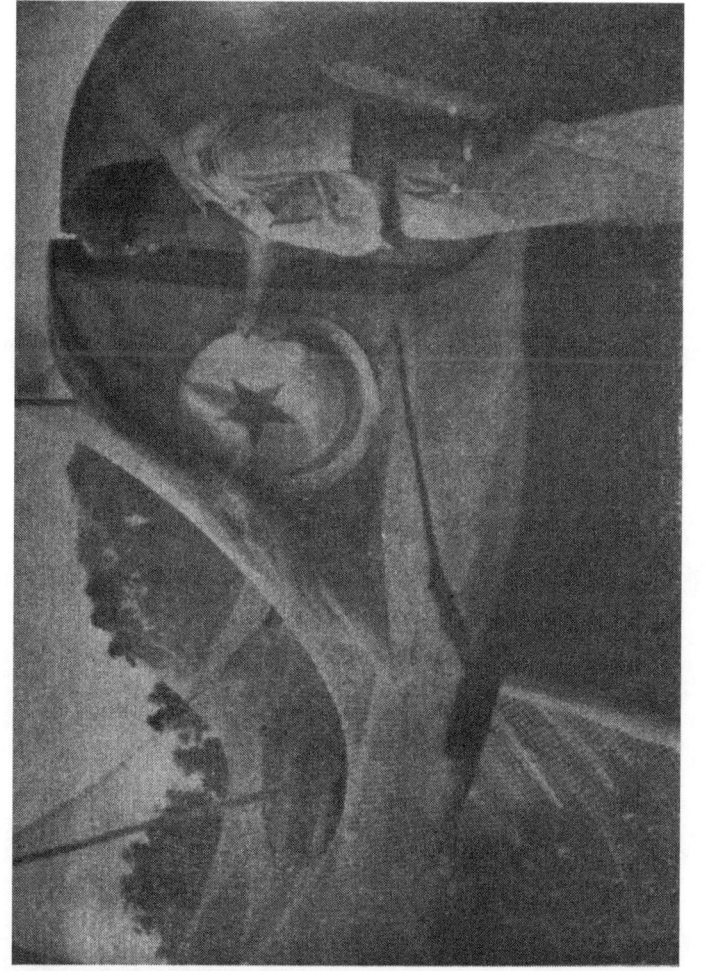

BIDAR AIRFIELD

Cardboard aircraft—Part of the Hyderabad Deception Plan.

across country. Fortunately also, Strike Force found that the very excellent airfield at Bidar had only been partially damaged by our own air action on the first day. One strip was in fact untouched. The airfield, however, was covered with all sorts of obstructions but these were easily removable provided labour was available. Lt Col Ram Singh, commanding Strike Force was rather at a loss at first to find the manpower to clear these obstructions, as naturally it was impolitic for the troops to do so as they had to guard the approaches to the airfield and later to search the town of Bidar. A little thought, however, gave him the solution. As the nearest building to the airfield was the Bidar Jail, Strike Force Commander had the jail opened, put all the convicts under a small escort, to work on clearing the airfield and himself went forward with his troops to clear the town of Bidar. By 1500 hrs the airfield was cleared sufficiently for a Dakota to land. By 1545 hrs Bidar itself had been cleared and it was found that in the Fort area a large number of rifles, guns, and ammunition were stored. This area was immediately sealed off. The 3 HS Inf who had been responsible for the defence of Bidar, had left in such a hurry that they had even neglected to pack up their Mess and their officers' kit. This Mess property and the officers' kit was taken over by 9 DOGRA and a few days later, after the surrender, was returned intact to their owners, much to the gratitude of 3 HS Inf.

The Surrender Ultimatum.

In the meantime, the GOC in C Southern Command, Lt Gen Maharaj Shri Rajendrasinhji, DSO, had broadcast a surrender ultimatum to Maj-Gen El-Edroos which read as follows:—

Personal from Gen Rajendrasinhji to Gen El-Edroos.

Firstly—You will have appreciated that a situation has now been reached which fairly indicates that militarily your task has become a hopeless one. Further resistance by your troops can only result in heavy and unnecessary loss of life

Secondly—Razakars and other hostile elements which have previously displayed considerable powers of resistance to my troops have been dispersed and disarmed in all sectors where they have been met. My forces are now situated so that they can enter Hyderabad at will from several directions.

Thirdly—I, therefore, demand of you in the interest of humanity and to save unnecessary and useless loss of life, to lay down your arms.

Fourthly—Please acknowledge to me at POONA and to my Comd at SADASEOPET on frequency 6600 Kcs and reply immediately.

It was thought that Gen El-Edroos would reply accepting this surrender ultimatum almost immediately. The leading troops of 1 Armd Bde were told to look out for Hyderabad Army representatives carrying white flags and to send them to Div HQ by the fastest means. It later transpired that Hyderabad Army HQ had never received this message, or if they did, never admitted to it.

In the morning the Divisional Commander went up as usual to contact the leading troops. After a discussion with Brig Verma regarding the action to be taken in case the Hyderabad Army surrendered that afternoon, he returned to Main Div HQ and gave the Army Commander the gist of the main events over the R/T. They were both agreed that the surrender was almost certain that day. After this conversation, with time hanging slightly heavily, the Divisional Commander decided to fly to Bidar in one of the Air OP Austers, to see for himself what was going on there. Bidar was reached at 1530 hrs, a very short flight, and it was a great pleasure to see the thorough way in which Lt Col Ram Singh was getting on with his job. Incidentally this was the first aircraft to land at Bidar after Sidney Cotton.

The flight back started at 1630 hrs and while flying back to his HQ from Bidar, the Divisional Commander saw a most extraordinary sight as the aircraft approached Main Div HQ. Almost every vehicle was flying an Indian Union flag and the normally quiet though busy Main Div HQ seemed to be celebrating some form of holiday. Groups of soldiers were seen standing about near the "Operations Room." There was obviously some form of "burra tamasha" going on. The excitement down below appeared to communicate itself to the pilot who on landing, cracked his undercarriage. Rather shaken, the Divisional Commander emerged limping slightly to be met by the GSO1, who stated that the Hyderabad Radio had announced the surrender of the Hyderabad Army at 1700 hrs. This had also been confirmed by Southern Command.

The enthusiasm was remarkable and all the brigade commanders with the exception of Brig Verma, appeared to have assembled at Div HQ. There was great excitement and every one appeared to be in high spirits. However, much still had to be done and plans made for the entry of troops into Hyderabad the next day. The excitement was suppressed and Main Div HQ set to work once more in planning the next day's moves. During the evening, the Army Commander confirmed on the RT that the Nizam had deposed the Laik Ali Cabinet, formed an interim cabinet and had agreed to the immediate return of Indian Union troops to Secunderabad. The Hyderabad Army had surrendered unconditionally.

Administration.

Even though the Hyderabad Army had surrendered and 1 Armd Div was to move into Secunderabad the next day without opposition, it was obviously essential that the move should be on a war basis. In war it pays to be suspicious even after victory has been achieved. It was thought possible that though the Hyderabad Army as a whole would not oppose the advance, some groups of regular troops possibly assisted by irregulars might take the opportunity of a slackening up on the part of the Indian Army, to do some damage before dispersing or surrendering. Therefore, once again all echelons were filled up, ammunition and petrol was replenished and by 2000 hrs in the evening, the Division from an administrative point of view, was ready, either for a peace move or, if necessary, for another battle.

Review of Operations—D plus 4 day.

As has been said before, it was obvious in the morning that the Hyderabad Army was not going to put up a last ditch stand. This was lucky in view of the fact that the country over which the second part of the advance had been conducted was better suited to a defensive battle and from the minefield met, it was obvious that some preparations, more thorough than those made previously, had been made for defence. For the first time also the Hindus were coming out in large numbers to greet the troops and their enthusiasm was remarkable. These civilians stated that the morale of the Hyderabad troops in Bidar and elsewhere had been very low, while a few Hyderabad troops who had surrendered themselves, stated that there had been wild dissensions between the regulars and irregulars. The Hyderabad Army had accused the Razakars of getting them into a mess while the Razakars had accused the Hyderabad Army of being unable to clear up the mess. What little co-operation there had been between these two groups at first had completely broken down. Once again for the first time, retaliatory action by the majority community against the minority community was seen in Bidar. Almost every Muslim had left Bidar town and fled to some tombs about 5 miles away and a certain amount of loot was going on. At Bidar there was a large American Baptist Mission and the American preachers here, who had met the Divisional Commander during his brief visit, were supplied with petrol and asked to go and restore confidence among the Muslims. In Bidar Fort itself a veritable arsenal had been found, stocked up with all sorts of equipment. Large quantity of uniforms were also discovered strewn about and the statement of the local civilians that the Hyderabad Army had dispersed the previous night in mufti clothing was more than substantiated.

Owing to a premature explosion in the Bidar Fort area while it was being cleared, our casualties this day had been 1 officer and 2 OR of the Engineers seriously injured and all three later died in hospital. Among the opposition, a few regulars had surrendered but otherwise there appeared to have been no casualties.

The brief war, as such, was over but the more thinking officers realised that the easiest part of operation " POLO " was done with; by far the hardest part was to follow. This was the restoration of normal conditions after the tremendous upheaval that had obviously taken place. The main burden of such restoration would fall on the troops and would keep them occupied in police duties which no soldier really likes. It would mean fanning out to all parts of the State, dealing with communal trouble, with Communist trouble and with labour trouble. It would mean the restoration of communications and acting in aid of civil power. Winning the " war " had only taken five and a half days; winning the " peace " would be a more long drawn out process with many of the hardships of war but without the privileges of glory.

CHAPTER XI

"D Plus 5 Day—18 Sep, 48"

The night of 17/18 September was a busy one for all concerned and few people had any sleep. A long series of instructions had issued from Southern Command who had got most of them from the Government of India. The collapse had been so sudden that Delhi itself was perhaps a little bewildered as to what to do immediately. These instructions were discussed between the BGS and the Divisional Commander, while points requiring clarification kept on being referred to the Army Commander. The moment was a great one and it was important that both the broad policy and the details should be correct. What was happening in Hyderabad itself was not clearly known. Razvi had broadcast perhaps the finest speech in his life, his renunciation speech. The Nizam had also broadcast and this aged but astute ruler had somewhat confused the issue by merely deposing the Laik Ali Cabinet, setting up a Cabinet of "stooges" and inviting the Indian troops back to Secunderabad. The Indian Agent-General, Mr. K. M. Munshi, just released from internment, was negotiating details as to how and when the Indian Army would come in. Both Commanders and Staff of 1 Armd Div all knew Hyderabad and the Cantonment area well which was a tremendous advantage on the making of the next day's plans. The result of such discussion were the orders that emanated from Southern Command and they can perhaps be best summed up in note form:

(a) Maj Gen J. N. Chaudhuri, under the orders of the GOC in C, Southern Command, was to accept the surrender of the Hyderabad Army, at a point 5 miles outside Hyderabad on the Secunderabad fork at 1200 hrs on the 18th September.

(b) Maj Gen Chaudhuri was to take over immediately the functions of Military Governor of Hyderabad State in addition to his duties as Commander, 1 Armd Div. As Military Governor his first task was to be the restoration of law and order.

(c) Immediately after the surrender, the Hyderabad Army was to come under command of Maj Gen Chaudhuri and it was left to his discretion as to how he should use them.

(d) Immediate orders to be issued by Maj Gen Chaudhuri on his assumption of Military Governorship were left to his discretion but he was to meet the Army Commander who was flying down to Bidar early on the morning of the 18th September and further discuss and clarify matters with him.

(e) As many troops as possible were to be moved into Secunderabad by the evening of 18th September.

(f) The Hyderabad Army, who had stated that the road forward of Sangareddipet had been extensively mined, was to send a mine clearing party to lift such mine fields by the time Indian Union troops arrived there. The Hyderabad Army was also to send guides to contact the leading troops at the surrender post.

(g) The civil element of the Military Government was to arrive for the day on 19th September, and have discussions with Maj Gen Chaudhuri after which they were to return to Poona and come back two days later permanently.

(h) Members of the Laik Ali Ministry were to be interned immediately.

(i) All leading Razakars were to be apprehended while Kasim Razvi, if still in Hyderabad, was to be arrested forthwith.

As a result of these orders, the Divisional Commander while naturally feeling elated was yet at the same time extremely anxious. Once again India had set a tremendous task to her troops and it was essential that this task should be carried out quickly and precisely. There were too many issues involved, both national and international, to allow for mistakes. Though no reports had been received of communal trouble starting up in Hyderabad City itself, the situation was obviously so inflammable that a wave of terror might start up at any time. Owing to the limitations of road space it was impossible to get more than one brigade into Secunderabad by nightfall. It was not considered sound to have troops moving after dark.

Consequently the following orders were issued. At first light, 1 Armd Bde Gp was to move to Bolarum preceded by a mine clearing party who were to keep on clearing the road until such time as the Hyderabad party working from the other side was contacted. Once the road was cleared they were to move into Bolarum as soon as possible. Provisional barrack allocations had already been given. Main HQ 1 Armd Div, still in control of operations, was to move to Sadaseopet. 7 Inf Bde Gp was to move to the vicinity of Sangareddipet, while 9 Inf Bde Gp was to move up to Sadaseopet. Rear HQ, 1 Armd Div was to move to the area vacated by 7 Inf Bde. Strike Force was to remain in

Kasim Razvi shortly after capture.

Bidar and help the Civil Administrator of that district, who was already in position at Homnabad, to control the area. The Divisional Commander was to meet the GOC in C, Southern Command, at Bidar airfield at 0715 hrs after which he was to move to the head of 1 Armd Bde column and take the surrender from Maj Gen El-Edroos at the time and place already indicated.

The morning of 18th September, dawned as a fine clear day but most of the Staff Officers and Commanders had been up well before dawn. The troops started to move forward at first light according to plan and the Divisional Commander with a reduced Tac HQ moved by Jeep to Bidar. Sharp at 0715 hrs the noise of an aircraft was heard and the RIAF Dakota carrying the GOC in C, Southern Command, and Air Vice Marshal S. Mukerjee, who had been in charge of air operations against Hyderabad, landed at Bidar airfield. A guard of honour had been found from 9 DOGRA and the GOC in C, Southern Command, deplaned and inspected the guard. Immediately after inspecting the guard, the whole party adjourned to the 9 DOGRA camp mess. Here, over cups of real troops tea, hot, strong and sweet, the plans for the day and the plans for the future were discussed briefly and hurriedly. There was not much time. A word must be said here to add to the laurels which have already been showered upon the Army Commander. Though really entitled to take the surrender himself, he had delegated it to the Divisional Commander of 1 Armd Div as a token of the regard he had for the troops who had done so much in this Hyderabad affair. This great gesture raised the already high esteem in which the Army Commander was held by the Armd Div, right up to the skies and gave a fine inspiration for other commanders to follow. As for the troops, they were delighted and the Army Commander's reward to the Division is still talked about.

After two cups of tea there was no time left for further discussions and the Army Commander wished the Divisional Commander the best of luck and told him to go ahead with his new job. He said that he himself would fly down with the Civilian Team the next day and meet him at Hakimpet. Though he could not advise in detail about the duties of a Military Governor, he hoped that commonsense and experience would be the guide. As far as he was concerned, in whatever was done, both himself and HQ Southern Command would back the decisions taken. This last, of course, gave tremendous confidence to everybody concerned. Finally, the Army Commander announced his decision to have a look at Bidar City itself and the troops nearby.

At 0800 hrs the Divisional Commander left Bidar and started to move to the head of the column. Wireless reports had been coming in from 1 Armd Bde that the progress of the advance was slow. No signs had been seen of the Hyderabad mine clearing party, while the haphazard placing of defensive mine fields along the road was taking a certain amount of finding and clearing. Arriving at the head of the column, the Divisional Commander made a rough estimate of time and space and reached the conclusion that at the present speed of advance he would not be able to get to the surrender spot at the time stipulated. The delay was being caused by the necessity to lift mines and repair minor demolitions. He wirelessed this information back to HQ Southern Command, and stated that he would probably reach the rendezvous by 1600 hrs that afternoon. Southern Command were asked to make arrangements to inform Hyderabad. Though the wireless frequencies of the Hyderabad Army were known, they would not reply when called on them. The telephone line which could have been tapped, was down. Apparently the only communication that existed was between the Government of India and the Agent-General by wireless. To make doubly certain, from the Division's point of view, an Auster aircraft of the Air OP flight was flown forward with a message to drop at the surrender spot, stating that the time of arrival would now be 1600 hrs. The slow and exasperating progress continued and though everybody was looking out for the Hyderabad mine clearing party, there were still no signs of them.

At 1100 hrs, suddenly from the rear of the column, escorted by our MPs, appeared a party of Hyderabad troops in three lorries, under command of an engineer officer and with the Hyderabad Provost Marshal. They stated that they had been sent to lead the Indian Union troops into Hyderabad. Their suggestion, however, was a futile one, in that it consisted of turning the whole column back about 20 miles and going down the Vikarabad road which in itself added a detour of 40 miles. Apparently the Vikarabad road had not been mined. As any soldier could have said, at this stage, it was quite impossible to turn the Division both for reasons of road space and morale. The Divisional Commander decided to continue to go forward, clearing up the mines with his own troops. The Hyderabad party, though sent to clear mines, had neither mine maps, equipment, nor any knowledge of where the mines had been laid.

This slow forward movement was perhaps the most exasperating part of the whole campaign. Victory had been won and yet the advance was slow and tiresome. Every quarter of a mile or so either mines would be found, or a bund would be seen to be demolished. The mines would have to be lifted, the road bulldozed back into place again and the advance would continue for another short hop. To speed up matters the Hyderabad mine clearing party were set to work to assist the Indian

THE SURRENDER

Maj Gen J. N. Chaudhuri (left) accepting on behalf of the GOC-in-C Southern Command, the surrender of the Hyderabad Army from Maj Gen S. A. El-Edroos,

Army. They were taken off very shortly afterwards, however, as it was found that their methods of clearance were either deliberately or unconsciously ineffective. The first section of the road which they declared clear and over which the leading Jeep was to pass, was found to have been only partially cleared. Two mines had been left and had the Divisional Commander gone forward he would certainly have been blown up. It was a lucky escape.

Finally the fork road outside Hyderabad was reached and here the Hyderabad mine clearing party stated that though they did not know much, they did know that forward of this point there were no demolitions or mine fields. Just to make certain however they were put in the lead along this road and closely followed by the Commander and his group. Their statement was correct and at 1600 hrs exactly the surrender spot was reached. Just before arriving here, the Divisional Commander had called up his various Group Commanders to be present at the surrender ceremony. After all, victory had not been won by any one man alone but by all and it was only just that representatives of all groups should see the surrender. Also, determined to maintain the smart reputation of the Indian Army, a mile before the surrender spot, the column was halted and all officers and ORs who were going to be present at the ceremony, got out their water bottles and towels and generally spruced themselves up. An American journalist who had reached the head of the column by then, took a photograph of these proceedings which he later sent to the Divisional Commander with his compliments. His caption was "just to prove to the world that the surrender was a clean job."

It had originally been said that HH the Prince of Berar, Mr. K. M. Munshi (Agent-General for India in Hyderabad) and the Commander of the Hyderabad Army, Maj Gen S. A. El-Edroos, would be present at the surrender ceremony. Later the composition of this party had been altered and only Maj Gen El-Edroos, with one aide, was present waiting to surrender his Army. General Chaudhuri got out of his Jeep and walked towards General El-Edroos. Both Commanders saluted punctiliously and his Group Commanders formed up in line behind General Chaudhuri. It was a very tense moment. General Chaudhuri said "I have been ordered by Lieut-Gen Maharaj Shri Rajendrasinhji, GOC in C, Southern Command, to take the surrender of your Army." General El-Edroos replied in a low voice "You have it." General Chaudhuri said "You understand that this surrender is unconditional." The answer was "Yes, I understand." General Chaudhuri then said "You understand that you and all troops of the Hyderabad Army now come under my command by virtue of the powers vested in me by the GOC in C, Southern Command." General El-Edroos once again replied "Yes."

After this the tension somewhat relaxed. General Chaudhuri pulled out his cigarette case and offered the defeated Commander a cigarette. Both of them lit up and after a little silence, General Chaudhuri started to give orders as to what was to be done. General El-Edroos was to go immediately and clear Bolarum and Secunderabad barracks of any Hyderabad troops he had there. These troops were to be moved before nightfall so that 1 Armd Bde could come into the area. The Hyderabad Army was to remain responsible for law and order within Hyderabad City until such time as the Indian Army was in a position to take over. General El-Edroos, who had been nominated as a member of the interim Cabinet, was to get members of the Government together and have them ready to meet General Chaudhuri at 1900 hrs that evening. He was also ordered to inform the IG Police, that curfew in all parts of Hyderabad was to be enforced from 1900 hrs to 0600 hrs till further orders and that police officers were also to take their instructions from the Military Governor.

On being asked about the communal situation in Hyderabad, General El-Edroos said that in the City itself there had been no trouble, though in the suburbs there had been some slight commotion but all was quiet now. Kasim Razvi had apparently not fled the State and his apprehension was immediately ordered. Edroos was dubious about what the effects of this would be but when promised the backing of some Indian troops, said he would arrange to arrest him. Razvi, frightened and with the bombast gone out of him, was duly delivered the next morning. He had been found at his brother-in-law's house, some way out of Hyderabad City. When found he had got a loaded revolver in his hand, which every five minutes he was putting to his head saying he would shoot himself. This gave the party out to arrest him some concern. Would he or would he not commit suicide as his captors came up? Not quite knowing what to do, the matter was referred back to the Divisional Commander. On discovering that Razvi had been sitting like this for the last twenty-four hours, orders were given to go ahead. Like any other bully, when properly tackled, his courage had evaporated. The behaviour of the Indian troops who were guarding him was most interesting. Before and during the operations, they were out for his blood. Once they had him, they completely ignored him. Cigarettes, tea and blankets to sleep on were given to Razvi and he was treated kindly. It just went to show what a fine gentleman the Indian soldier was. If the situation had been reversed, what would have been their fate !

After the surrender, the whole party drove to the house of Mr. K. M. Munshi, the Agent-General for India in Hyderabad, and found a most exuberant crowd of citizens waiting. Once again short discussions were held. Munshi was asked as to what had been happening, but, it

DECCAN HOUSE

Maj Gen J. N. Chaudhuri and Mr. K. M. Munshi meet, just after the surrender. Over K. M. Munshi's left shoulder can be seen Swami Ramanand Tirth, the President of the local State Congress Party.

had been made quite clear to the Divisional Commander that he and he alone was responsible for further action to be taken in Hyderabad. General Chaudhuri had already handed over officiating command of the Division to his senior Brigadier, Brigadier Verma, commanding 1 Armd Bde Group. It was clearly apparent, that if the Divisional Commander had to carry out the functions of a Military Governor he would not be able to command the Division adequately as well. Brigadier Verma who knew Hyderabad, had already worked out an accommodation plan and Secunderabad was full of the noise of tracked and wheeled vehicles moving in an orderly way to their ordered destinations. The noise of their passage was almost covered by the cheers of the populace. The scenes of enthusiasm were terrific. There was not a single armoured or other vehicle which had not got a crowd of citizens festooned around it. Army officers only had to appear on the road to be loudly cheered, while officers in Jeeps were almost mobbed with affection. As dusk drew on and the curfew order came into operation, the crowds started to disperse. The steady movement of vehicles however went on but by nightfall a still silence was settling all over the State.

Commanders and staffs were however working furiously. On the military side the next day's moves were being planned. Some troops had to come into Secunderabad, others were to go out to the districts. The logistical problem in itself was terrific. On the Military Government side, the activity was equally furious. However, as writers say that is another story and perhaps may be written up later. At midnight that night a tired but happy Tac Div HQ—Tac Div HQ no longer but the nucleus of the Military Governor's HQ—sat down to dinner at the Lake View Guest House where they had established themselves for the night. Obviously a celebration was indicated but everyone was too tired to celebrate in the traditional manner. The celebration could therefore wait until the whole job had been done. The first part of the " Police Action " was over. What would the second part bring?

CHAPTER XII

LESSONS LEARNT

"POLO" cannot in any sense be called a major war but there is no doubt that certain detailed operations of war were executed. Though opposition from the enemy was limited, badly controlled and sporadic, this did not in any way affect the precision with which planning, the actual control of operations and administration on our side had to be done. When operations were being planned, the degree of resistance to be met was not known. In fact, if the majority of India was to be believed, resistance was going to be considerable and what is more well led. The campaign had to be planned throughout with the thought of meeting the stiffest resistance while during all stages of the execution this thought had to be kept continually in view. As a result of this policy, apart from commanders and staffs, particularly the junior ones, receiving the best possible training, had the Hyderabad army conducted their operations better, there would have been NO necessity to make any major changes. There would have been no disorganisation, no sudden demands on an already depleted Command HQ for such items as reinforcements, short notice supply by air, more transport and the many other things that throw policy out of joint and lead to delay and futility. Also, the troops taking part were continually on the alert and this in itself was no mean asset. It is fair to say that even if Hyderabad had put up the strongest resistance of which she was capable, the ultimate result could only have been delayed by two days. There has always been much discussion as to whether war is an art or a science. The genius of the artist undoubtedly plays a large part, particularly in the planning. But, without the meticulous precision of the scientist in execution, success becomes a matter of luck and any Commander who relies on luck is only gambling.

There is no doubt that the success of these operations was also largely due to the very careful planning and the dissemination of such plans at all levels. Few people can make a complete plan by themselves and free discussions between selected experts, working on a general premise is necessary before a good plan can be born. Except for reasons of extreme speed or other dire necessity, it is always unwise to foist a plan on a commander without getting his reaction to it first. After all, he will have to execute the plan and, should he not be convinced of its intrinsic soundness, his execution can only be half-hearted or uninspired. Where possible a senior subordinate commander should be allowed to make his own detailed plan based on the general framework.

If confidence is reposed in the commander, there should be no interference of how he utilises his own resources, though the final plan must be checked, while he should be encouraged to ask for help which must be freely given. If little confidence is reposed in the commander, he should go at once; it is fairest to him, his superiors and most of all the troops he commands. Successful planning can only be done in an atmosphere of cordiality with even perhaps occasional lapses to ribaldry. Seldom can any operations have been planned at all levels, in such a friendly spirit as that in which operation POLO was planned in Southern Command. The effects of this had its repercussions throughout, cordiality giving confidence meaning success. Another point which is so much talked about but so often badly done, is the correct dissemination of plans. Within the limits of security, not only the plan but the commander's intention and his general policy must be known to all those taking part down to the lowest ranks, before operations start. Security is vital, particularly at the higher levels and in the early stages. Against that, troops, who go into battle knowing nothing of the overall picture and what the ultimate object is, are troops badly equipped. The well trained soldier can be made most security conscious.

The lessons discussed above are general lessons, applicable in any series of operations but also receiving full emphasis in this one. Certain particular lessons emerge, however, which are of considerable interest. Though the Armoured Division normally consists of an armoured brigade and a lorried brigade, in some cases an extra infantry brigade is also put under command. This was so in this case. It was the first time, however, that a force of the strength as constituted above, had taken part in an Indian theatre of battle and had operated in this particular type of terrain. For the operation of tanks and mobile troops, the limitations of such a terrain are obvious. There is a shortage of roads and the main operation has usually to be conducted along one particular road. Roads are narrow and though normally two-way, for this type of force can only be considered as one-way. Surfaces are poor and liable to break up very quickly. Bridges are narrow and of low carrying capacity, while the streams they bridge are dry with sandy banks and beds. The bigger streams usually have one deep channel in them at all times of the year. In the rains such rivers are unfordable. The surrounding country in the dry weather is usually good for tracks but bad for wheels because of the bunds. In the rainy season, four months of the year, the going, particularly in paddy and black cotton soil, is extremely difficult. Distances between main civil centres are large, so that diversions and raids have to cover long distances. Local resources for any purpose, whether it be supplies or bridging material is extremely limited. Lines of Communication facilities are always extremely meagre, bases difficult of preparation, while the single road and single railway, the latter not always available, make maintenance and evacuation the two biggest problems the commander has to contend with. Available airfields to support are few and far between. The Armoured Division thrust got its limited air support from as far back as Poona, one hour's fighter flying distance from the scene of operations. Maps for detailed planning are on a small scale, sometimes out of date and sometimes inaccurate when giving a picture of the countryside.

All these difficulties are enhanced by the attitude of the local population. Where they are hostile for either a communal or ideological reason, they will actively try to sabotage troop movements, maintenance movements and security. This sabotage at its worst can be well controlled and dangerous. Even where the population is friendly, lack of education makes them panicky, prone to exaggerate reports and to give information based on improving their own security rather than helping the troops. Every effort may and probably will be made to divert troops, with tales of atrocities in centres well away from the main line of advance. Whether friendly or hostile, there is always the danger of a big refugee problem, once again cluttering up the few roads available. Such refugees and also villagers who have not moved can present a serious problem to the troops, in the spreading of disease together with the necessity for feeding them and looking after their sanitation. The political implications in dealing with civilians have always to be remembered.

The one consolation in this enumeration of handicaps to the advancing troops, is that the defenders are faced with similar problems. They will be unable to move reserves quickly, their lines of withdrawal may well be choked by refugees, while the problem of dealing with a panicky civil population must play a large part in their basic strategy.

Based on the above, certain lessons emerge and perhaps for the sake of clarity and brevity, it is best to tabulate them:—

> (a) Under Indian conditions, not more than one division can operate along a single road. Under the best circumstances such a road can only have two brigades on the move at the same time; road space conditions will not permit maintenance and the movement of three motorised brigades. At the worst, movement will be confined to the leading troops only, probably a regimental group with some other arms under command. Neglecting this lesson in an effort to move too much too far, will lead to a complete maintenance breakdown,

(b) It is wrong to advance on or accept too wide a front, particularly on a divisional level. Distances and lack of communications will make control extremely difficult, while the problem of maintenance and the guarding of the L of C will be much accentuated. Movement on too wide a front must also inevitably slow down forward movement and fritter away troops on the security of the L of C. The plan should aim at a strong, concentrated, deep thrust from a firm base to a strategical key point. From here, after drawing one's tail in and "tidying it up," another concentrated deep thrust must go in. Remember that the defender is originally at a disadvantage as he must accept a certain amount of dispersion. Lack of communications will limit the number of strategical key points and it is better to be there in strength before the enemy has concentrated.

(c) If detachments off the main axis have to be made, such detachments should be strong, composed of all arms and administratively secure. The commander should be chosen for his ability and be given plenty of scope, scope stopping just short of an independent command. The divisional commander cannot be looking all ways at once and his chief task must always be to concentrate on the main axis of advance.

(d) The bold handling of artillery is essential and at the possible risk of exposing them, to get the fullest effect, they must be concentrated well forward. Otherwise when they are needed they will be far down the column, with the resultant waste of time in getting them up and deploying them. In the handling of artillery it is the weight of shell on a single important target that counts and not the number of targets that are engaged. It will be noted that in operation "POLO," the heaviest guns available, one battery of medium guns (5.5 in), were grouped with STRIKE FORCE, the leading group.

(e) Some bridging material, the types and quantities based on what is to be met, should be held well forward, at the expense of taking up the road space of other arms. Arrangements must exist to get it speedily to the spot where it is required even if this means halting every other vehicle. In the long run the results will be quicker. To achieve speed, the correct utilisation of engineer resources and their correct grouping is essential. In making the engineer part of the plan, accurate intelligence is necessary and should be obtained from maps, air-photos, meteorological reports and local knowledge. Based on these factors a sound appreciation and plan must be made.

(*f*) Commanders should be ruthless in cutting down the number of vehicles permitted to each unit during the operations. This cutting down must certainly be done at the expense of anything considered a luxury and all ranks must be trained to and be prepared to live very hard. The present War Establishments based on American lease-lend and a Middle Eastern or European theatre of war, are generous and unit commanders will plead for every vehicle. The formation commander must however be quite clear in his own mind as to what he wants forward and what can come up later. Note the Armd Div's introduction of a ' D ' echelon. This cutting down of vehicles to gain road space may even take into consideration, the cutting down of ammunition and other stores carried. In operation " POLO " the first line ammunition of the tanks was cut down to save road space.

(*g*) With the limited air support available at present, commanders and troops must not continually expect or suddenly ask for air support and air supply. Any plans made should be workable without either of these two factors. Where air support is available, it should be utilised economically keeping a reserve of sorties for emergency. Suitable tasks would always be Tac R plus the " shooting up " of any movement seen in enemy held territory. Where the enemy has a strong air force, it must be the duty of the AOC in charge of the operations, after gaining air superiority to try and neutralise the enemy planes and try and give fighter cover to our advancing troops.

(*h*) Once again with limited road space, inaccurate maps and possible lack of local intelligence that may be encountered, the attachment of an Air OP flight to each division is advocated. Where an Air OP flight is available, apart from the normal tasks, they can be used for reporting the progress of the advance, reporting the progress of a battle, reporting on roads, bridges, and country over which the troops will have to advance, and the evacuation of serious casualties if necessary. Their utilisation as " VIP taxis " is the last use to which they should be put. In most parts of India, it is easy to find a suitable site and with a motor grader make a satisfactory light airstrip within two hours. Where such an airstrip has been made, the position of Main Div HQ should be adjacent.

(i) Where there is an air threat, during certain periods of the operations, movement will be possible only by night and all troops must be trained in this, particularly the armour. Armoured unit and sub-unit commanders are chary of night movement but this prejudice must be overcome. What is equally important also is that neither night or day should affect maintenance. RIASC columns should be prepared to move and issue at night. Repair and recovery should be practised by dark. Getting into harbour after nightfall should be a common place.

(j) In operations over this terrain, the fighting troops should be self-contained as far as possible particularly with regard to petrol and rations. Experience has shown that each B vehicle can easily carry 200 miles reserve of petrol and 3 days hard rations for the occupants. Reserves should not be eaten into indiscriminately and a good rule is to allow 50 per cent to be touched only under the brigade commander's orders and the other 50 per cent only under the divisional commander's orders. A vehicles cannot carry any reserves on the vehicle itself but their POL reserves are catered for on the establishment and vehicles carrying such reserves must be held well forward. The advantages of carrying such reserves are obvious as where road space is limited on a particular day, the only maintenance columns moving need be the ammunition columns.

(k) All infantry should be used to working with tanks, a point sometimes forgotten, while in any particular operation, the actual infantry to work with the tanks should be previously " married up " to units and sub-units.

(l) To get maximum utilisation of road space, MT discipline must be perfect and this can only be obtained in war if it obtains in peace. Drivers must have it as second nature to pull right off the road when they halt, to keep the correct laid down distances when moving, to make the correct signals when on the move and to know exactly what to do from the tactical point of view if a breakdown occurs. Orders for action against hostile air attack must be clearly laid down and each individual must know what he is to do. Another point often forgotten is that each driver must know where the column is going so that in case he gets separated he does not lose himself. Officers should patrol their unit column on motorcycles and it is better that an officer when travelling in a vehicle, sits at the back with his men where he can see what is going on rather than sitting in front comfortably with the driver. Hoods and canopies must always be up.

(m) For such mobile operations there is no need to emphasise the importance of traffic control. In the long run, traffic control is an operational matter and should be dealt with by the 'G' staff rather than by the A/Q staff. The facilities available with Divisional Provost on present establishments, make it quite impossible for them to carry out their traffic control duties efficiently and in a co-ordinated manner. They will always have to be helped out. At the risk of taking a much needed officer away from his unit, it is better to locally appoint a GSO_2 (Traffic) at Div HQ for control while the actual physical traffic control and the inter-communications involved may well be made the responsibility of some unit HQ which is not being employed fully during that particular phase of operations. The HQ LAA Regt can usually be used for this purpose or else the HQ of the Light Armd Regt, if they are not actually in the lead.

(n) Though it is the normal duty of maintenance convoys moving up and down a road to protect themselves, where intrusions on the L of C are expected, this protection must be stepped up. Two methods can be used. Firstly, the picketing of all roads and tracks leading in to the main line of communication as well as the guarding of defiles. This method is wasteful of troops but is essential where the threat to communications is known to be strong. Secondly, the allotment of specific troops from fighting units for convoy protection. It may even be necessary to take one squadron from the Light Armd Regt for this task. A combination of the two methods perhaps gives the best protection of all.

(o) In mobile operations, the maintenance plan must always be worked out in the greatest detail and cases may occur where maintenance considerations may limit tactical moves. Remember that no maintenance means no movement. The commander should also limit his advance in accordance with the plans previously made. This may be an irritation where resistance turns out to be unexpectedly weak but the danger of ignoring this principle may mean a longer delay later and what is worse, suddenly encountering the enemy in strength when the lines of communication are overstretched. In these lessons, no mention has been made of the other principles of administration as they are expressed better and in more detail in the text-books. Avoid improvisation and stick to normality; where improvisation is unavoidable, base it firmly on principles.

(*p*) In operation "POLO" the intercept service formed at Divisional HQ was most effective. Though such interception is not normally done on a Divisional level, in Eastern theatres the long distances involved and the need for intercepts to get to the fighting commanders as soon as possible, make the provision of such an intercept service worthy of consideration.

(*q*) In any operations to-day there is always a political aspect. Commanders must be fully told their responsibility in this direction particularly with reference to the treatment and control of the civil population and civil installations. Where commanders feel they have not been sufficiently briefed in this matter by their superior commanders, they should insist on getting exact instructions in this respect in writing. They should also know whether any civil officials would be available to them for dealing with such problems thus freeing commanders for the main task of fighting the battle. The economic breakdown of an invaded country during a war can be largely minimised by clear orders on this subject together with the immediate posting of trained civil officials to take over administration in occupied enemy territory. Based on the above, a commander must at all times strictly control the action of his troops with regard not only to the civil population but also with regard to installations, public amenities, buildings, plants and other such important things captured during the advance. In the training period, all ranks should be thoroughly indoctrinated with what they have to do with regard to such matters.

In the preface it has been emphasised that the lessons given above are based on broad principles and in some cases are a repetition of well-known principles. However, the preparation for and the execution of "POLO," brought out these lessons over and over again. If this re-emphasis has served to firmly embed these lessons in the minds of readers, the object has been achieved.

Appx A to 1 Armd Div in Op "Polo"

LOCATION STATEMENT AS AT 31 JUL 48

Ser No	Unit	Location
	HQ	
1	HQ 1 Armd Div	..POONA
2	HQ 1 Armd Div Arty	..AUNDH
3	HQ 623 Army Engr Gp	..POONA
4	HQ 1 Armd Div Regt RIASC	.. ,,
5	HQ 1 Armd Div CIEME	.. ,,
6	HQ 1 Armd Div CIAOC	.. ,,
	ARTY	
7	1 Fd Regt (SP)	..AUNDH
8	9 Para Fd Regt (towed)	..DIGHI
9	34 (M) A Tk Regt (SP)	..AUNDH
10	2 Indep Air OP Flt	..POONA
11	26 LAA Regt less two btys	..DIGHI
12	One bty 40 Med Regt	..AUNDH
13	Det 20 Svy Regt	..DEOLALI
	ENGRS	
14	7 Fd Coy	..DIGHI
15	10 Fd Coy	..BIJAPUR
16	65 Fd Coy	..SHOLAPUR
17	11 Fd Pk Coy	..KIRKEE
	SIGS	
18	1 Armd Div Sig Regt	..POONA
19	1 Armd Bde Sig Coy	..AHMEDNAGAR
20	7 Inf Bde Sig Sec	..SHOLAPUR
21	9 Inf Bde Sig Sec	..BIJAPUR
22	1 Fd Regt Sig Sec	..AUNDH
23	9 Para Fd Regt Sig Sec	..DIGHI
24	1 HORSE Sig Sec	..SHOLAPUR
25	3 CAV Sig Sec	..AHMEDNAGAR
26	17 HORSE Sig Sec less det	,,
27	26 LAA Regt Sig Sec less dets	DIGHI
28	34(M) A Tk Regt Sig Sec	..AUNDH
	BDES	
29	HQ 1 Armd Bde	,,AHMEDNAGAR

Ser No	Unit	Location	
30	1 HORSE	..SHOLAPUR	
31	3 CAV	..AHMEDNAGAR	
32	17 HORSE less one sqn	,,	
33	9 DOGRA less one coy	,,	One coy JAMKHED
34	HQ 7 Inf Bde	..SHOLAPUR	
35	3 IND GRS	..POONA	
36	14 RAJPUT	..NANAJ	
37	2 R SIKH less one coy	..SHOLAPUR	one coy BARSI
38	HQ 9 Inf Bde	..BIJAPUR	
39	3 PUNJAB less two coys	..BAGALKOT	One coy RON One coy HUNGUND
40	1 BIHAR	..DUDHANI	
41	2/1 GR less one coy	..HIPPARGI	One coy TALIKOTA

RIASC

42	93 Comp Pl	..SHOLAPUR	
43	105 Comp Pl	..BIJAPUR	
44	108 Comp Pl	..AHMEDNAGAR	
45	116 Comp Pl	..POONA	
46	631 Coy RIASC (Bde Gp)	..SHOLAPUR	
47	632 Coy RIASC (Bde Gp)	..DHOND	One pl at DEOLALI
48	636 Coy RIASC (Bde Gp)	..BIJAPUR	
49	649 Coy RIASC (Div Tps)	..POONA	
50	653 Coy RIASC (Tk Tptr)	..AHMEDNAGAR	

MED

51	84 Fd Amb	..BIJAPUR	
52	85 Fd Amb	..SHOLAPUR	
53	9 Lt Fd Amb	..POONA	
54	1 Lt Fd Hyg Sec less three sub secs	..KIRKEE	One Sub Sec AHMEDNAGAR
55	2 Fd Surg T	..SHOLAPUR	
56	6 Fd Surg T	..POONA	

IEME

57	HQ 7 Inf Bde LAD type I	..SHOLAPUR	
58	HQ 9 Inf Bde LAD type I	..BIJAPUR	
59	1 HORSE LAD type III	..SHOLAPUR	
60	3 CAV LAD type III	..AHMEDNAGAR	
61	17 HORSE LAD type III less det	,,	
62	1 Fd Regt (SP) LAD type III	..AUNDH	
63	9 Para Fd Regt LAD type II	..DIGHI	
64	34(M) A Tk Regt (SP) LAD type III	..AUNDH	
65	11 Fd Pk Coy LAD type II	..KIRKEE	

Ser No	Unit	Location	
66	1 Armd Div Sigs LAD type II	..POONA	
67	5 Armd Wksp Coy ..	..AHMEDNAGAR	
68	1 Armd Bde Rec Coy less two dets	,,	
69	120 Inf Wksp Coy less one sec	..SHOLAPUR	One sec BIJAPUR
70	128 Inf Wksp Coy ..	..AUNDH	
71	1033 Tpt Coy Wksp Sec	..SHOLAPUR	for 631 Coy
72	1046 Tpt Coy Wksp Sec	..DEOLALI	for 632 Coy
73	1187 Tpt Coy Wksp Sec	..POONA	for 649 Coy
74	1188 Tpt Coy Wksp Sec	..AHMEDNAGAR	for 653 Coy
75	One sec 5 Div Tpt Coln Wksp	..BIJAPUR	for 636 Coy
76	103 Indep Rec Sec ..	..POONA	
77	Det 26 LAA Regt Wksp	..DIGHI	

ORD

78	1 Armd Div Ord Fd Pk less det	KIRKEE	

INT

79	569 F S Sec ..	SHOLAPUR	

PRO

80	1 Armd Div Pro unit less two secs and one det	..POONA	

Appx B to 1 Armd Div in Op "POLO"
ARMS AND AMMUNITION BROUGHT BY SIDNEY COTTON

A Tk mines	1,000
Mor 2 in	8
Mor 3 in	10
Bombs mor 2 in	2,500
.50 Browning amn	5,000
Shells 25 pr HE	500
AA gun OERLIKON	1
A Tk guns 6 pr	6
*TSMGs	1,000
TSMG amn	5,00,000
.303 rifles	10,000
.303 amn	5,00,000
**BARETTA SMCs	3,000
BARETTA amn	10,01,000

* Thomson Sub Machine Gun.
** Sub Machine Carbine.

Appx C to 1 Armd Div in Op "POLO"

COMPOSITION OF FORCES

Forces operating will be divided for convenience into the following five gps. The composition of these gps may be varied to suit particular ops should the need arise.

STRIKE FORCE Comd: Lt Col RAM SINGH

Tps : 1 HORSE less one sqn
One tp SHERMANS from HQ 1 Armd Div
One bty 1 Fd Regt (SP)
Det engrs
9 DOGRA less one coy
One VCP
Two amb cars to be detailed by ADMS.

SMASH FORCE Comd: Brig S. D. VERMA

Tps : 1 Armd Bde Gp
One tp of STUARTS from recce tp 1 HORSE
3 CAV less one sqn
1 Fd Regt (SP) less one bty
2 Bty 40 Med Regt
7 Fd Coy

One coy 9 DOGRA
One coy 85 Fd Amb
Det 1 Armd Bde Rec Coy
Det 5 Armd Bde Wksp Coy
One sec 1 Armd Div Pro Coy

Main HQ 1 Armd Div Gp :—
Main HQ 1 Armd Div
HQ Arty
One comp inf coy formed from 34 (M) A Tk Regt HQ 623 Engr Gp

       Main Div Sigs
       1 Armd Div Pro coy less dets
       569 F S Sec
       One sub sec 1 Fd Hyg Sec.

KILL FORCE ... **Comd**: Brig GURBACHAN SINGH

    Tps: HQ 7 Inf Bde
       9 Para Fd Regt
       One bty 34(M) A Tk Regt (SP)
       65 Fd Coy
       2 R SIKH
       3 IND GRS
       14 RAJPUT
       Det 1 Armd Bde Rec Coy
       Det 128 Inf Wksp Coy
       85 Fd Amb less one coy
       6 Fd Surg T
       One sub sec 1 Fd Hyg Sec
       One sec 1 Armd Div Pro Coy

Rear Div ... **Comd**: Lt Col GURCHARAN SINGH

    Tps: Rear HQ 1 Armd Div
       One sqn 1 HORSE
       HQ 1 Armd Div Regt RIASC, CIEME and CIAOC
       Rear Div Sigs
       26 LAA Regt less two btys
       11 Fd Pk Coy
       93, 108, 116, 105 Comp Pls
       631, 632, 636, 649, 653 Coys RIASC less dets otherwise emp.
       9 Lt Fd Amb
       84 Fd Amb less one coy
       2 Fd Surg T
       1 Fd Hyg Sec less two sub secs
       5 Armd Wksp Coy less det
       1 Armd Bde Rec Coy less dets
       120 Inf Wksp Coy less det
       128 Inf Wksp Coy less det
       103 Indep Rec Sec
       1 Armd Div OFP
       One sec 1 Armd Div Pro unit

VIR FORCE .. **Comd :** Brig APJI RANDHIR SINGH

Tps : HQ 9 Inf Bde
10 Fd Coy
3/2 PUNJAB
2/1 GR
One coy 84 Fd Amb
Det 5 Inf Div Pro Coy
One sec 120 Inf Wksp Coy

Notes

All arty and engrs though shown under gp headings will be under comd of those gps for mov and replenishment only. For ops they will op under the C Arty and CRIE respectively and will be in sp of the armour and inf. The services units shown in Rear Div Gp will also be centralised under their respective heads and therefore in sp, though the dets shown in other gps will be under comd.

Appx D to 1 Armd Div in Op "POLO"

"EXERCISE SHIVAJI"

SECRET
No. 1826-Q
Copy————

6 Aug 48

1 ARMD DIV MOV ORDER No 2

Ref SOUTHCOM ADM ORDER No 3 OF 16 JUN 48.

Ref maps: 47 F, 47 J, 47 M, 47 O one inch to four miles.

INFM

1. Units mentioned in Appx 'A' will move from POONA to SHOLAPUR by rd on 7 Aug on timings given.
2. All Div units in AHMEDNAGAR and 632 Coy RIASC at DHOND will be under comd 1 Armd Bde for rd/rail moves to SHOLAPUR.
3. All convoys will halt at Staging Camp TEMBHURNI for one night arriving SHOLAPUR the following day.

METHOD

4. Adv parties of NOT more than two vehs per unit will proceed direct to SHOLAPUR on 'S' day (the day conc starts) halting the night at TEMBHURNI. These parties will be self sufficient and under Comd DQ 1 Armd Div.

5. **Routes**

    (a) For convoys from POONA

	Miles
POONA—TEMBHURNI	97
TEMBHURNI—SHOLAPUR	53

    (b) For convoys from AHMEDNAGAR

AHMEDNAGAR—JALGAON UE $_{3565}$	89
KARMALA UE $_{4536}$ TEMBHURNI	89
TEMBHURNI—SHOLAPUR	53

6. **VTM**

   40 vtm

7. **Speed**

   30 mi2h

8. **Halts**

   Normal halts of 20 mins every 2 hrs finishing at even numbered clock hr will be observed by all convoys even at SP. Extra timing has been allotted to units that may have to halt at SP. First halt 0740 hrs to 0800 hrs. Long halts of one hr will be observed after 6 hrs running.

9. **SP**

   Rd/rail crossing—SHOLAPUR rd 9852. For timings for crossing SP see Appx 'A.'

10. All timings and distances will be strictly conformed to by units. To avoid congestion at SP, units will ensure that they cross the SP at the exact time allotted.

11. **TC**

    1 Armd Div Pro will est TCP at following places :—

    (a) SP
    (b) Junc of rds from AHMEDNAGAR and POONA at TEMBHURNI
    (c) Dis P at TEMBHURNI
    (d) Dis P at SHOLAPUR
    (e) TC from Dis P at SHOLAPUR to camp responsibility of SHOLAPUR Sub Area.

12. **Arms and amn**

    Personal arms and amn will be carried by all.

13. NO sec line amn will be drawn at POONA. This will be drawn at SHOLAPUR on arrival.

ADM

14. **Sups**

    All units will carry 2 days rations for the journey and 3 days res.

15. Ice for unit heat stroke centres will be sup from local purchase or from POONA.

16. Emergency ration and special packed compo rations will be drawn at destination.
17. Units will cook with kerosene cookers.
18. **POL**

    Units will start off with full tks and sufficient petrol for the journey to destination. No petrol will be drawn at Staging Camp.
19. 2nd line petrol will be drawn at destination.
20. Res pet as laid down will be carried.
21. **Canteens**

    Units may take own contractors with them to SHOLAPUR provided NO cost is incurred by Govt and on the understanding that the contractors may NOT be allowed to go further fwd at the discretion of Comd 1 Armd Div. This also holds good for civ servants.
22. **Tentage**

    Units will carry full scale of tentage only up to SHOLAPUR. Beyond SHOLAPUR tentage will be carried as per 1 Armd Div Op Order No. 2 of 16 Jul 48. Surplus tentage will be left at SHOLAPUR in charge of Sub Area.
23. **Water**

    Units will move with all water containers/trlrs full.
24. Water will be drawn from authorised sources only and will NOT be consumed without chlorination.
25. **Med**

    Hosp (50 beds) will be est in civ hosp SHOLAPUR by S plus 1.
26. Evac of cas by rd and rly.
27. All units maint own heat stroke stas in conc area.
28. Central heat stroke stas est at SHOLAPUR Hosp
29. Div units will conform to SHOLAPUR Indep Sub Area med and hyg orders.
30. Normal hot weather precautions will be observed.

31. **Rec**

    (a) 1 Armd Bde will send one wksp and rec det to TEMBHURNI on S day to remain in posn till Div conc is completed. It will rejoin the Div at SHOLAPUR on completion move of all Div units. This rec sec will move with adv party as mentioned in para 4 above.

    (b) Veh cas repairable in 2nd line will be evac fwd to Comd area. Remainder by easiest method, rd or rly to RVP DEHU.

32. **Rail moves**

    Policy—All wheels by rd, trs by rail. Except 24 tks of 1 Armd Bde which will move by rd on tk tptr of 653 Tk Tptr Coy.

33. For rail mov order see HQ MC Group POONA No. 3716/11 Q(M) of 28 Jul 48 fwd under this HQ No. 1907-Q of 29 Jul 48.

34. **Staging Camp**

    Following Staff will be provided at TEMBHURNI by HQ 1 Armd Div. This will be in posn by 1300 hrs on S minus 1.

    1 offr to be detailed by 'G' Branch.

    1 clerk to be detailed by 'G' Branch.

    5 OR to be detailed by OC Div Pro Unit.

    1 Sub Sec 1 Fd Hyg Sec.

    The duties of this staff will be :—

    (a) Allotment of Camping space for units from POONA and AHMEDNAGAR.

    (b) Water drawing programme.

    (c) Supervision hyg and sanitation of camp area.

    (d) TC for incoming and outgoing convoys.

    (e) Co-ord of move of units into and out of TEMBHURNI.

    This party will join Div on completion conc at new area without further orders.

35. Convoy Comd will arrange to send unit guides (one per unit) to report to Staging Camp offr at TEMBHURNI at least two hrs before arrival of convoys to recce area allotted and guide their units into the area from Dis P.

36. Personnel who can NOT go by rd may proceed by ordinary train service by arrangements with RTO POONA direct.

37. **Protection**

Convoy Comds are responsible for local protection of convoy.

INTERCOMN

38. By telephone between   (a) POONA-AHMEDNAGAR
                                    (b) POONA-SHOLAPUR

    Wrls between   (a) POONA-SHOLAPUR and TEMBHURNI.

ACK

                                    Sd/- HAR PARSAD
                                              Lt Col
                                        AA and QMG

Methods——SDS
Time of signature——1430
Time issued to Sigs——1450

Distribution :—

    1 Armd Bde
    3 IND GRS
    Arty
    Engrs
    Sigs
    ST
    Med
    Ord
    EME
    Pro
    HQ Sqn
    GS
    A
    South Comd
    POONA Sub Area
    SHOLAPUR (I) Sub Area
    7 Inf Bde
    9 Inf Bde
    SSD POONA

APPX 'A' to 1 ARMD DIV MOV ORDER No 2 of 6 AUG 48   SECRET

1. Date of Move 7 Aug 48
2. SP Rd rail crossing 9852 SHOLAPUR rd.
3. Density 40 vtm
4. Speed 30 (m/2h)
5. Location of reg HQ TEMBHURNI
6. Halts 20 mins every 2 hrs finishing at even numbered clock hr.
7. Staging area TEMBHURNI
8. Routes SHOLAPUR Rd.

Ser No	Fmn/Unit	Unit Distin-guishing No.	Number of vehs	TPP plus 50%	Route to Sp	Pass SP Head	Pass SP Tail	(Spare)	Spare	Remarks
(a)	(b)	(c)	(d)	(e)	(f)	(g)	(h)	(i)	(j)	(k)
1	7 INF BDE	..								
	3 IND GRS	60	32			0600	0605	..	..	Gp Comd to be detailed by 3 GRS
			32							
2	1 ARMD DIV (Main Gp)									
	Main HQ 1 Armd Div	40	33							Gp Comd to be detailed by HQ 1 Armd Div
3	34 A Tk Regt	77	16							
4	1 Armd Div Sigs	40	123	22		0615	0637	..	..	
5	1 Lt Fd Hyg Sec (less Sub Sec)	93	..							
			179							
6	26 LAA Regt (less two btys)	73	46							Gp Comd to be detailed by 26 LAA Regt
7	Det Pro unit	43	4	10		0645	0655	..	..	
			50							

xiv

1. Date of Move 8 Aug 48.
2. SP Rd rail crossing 9852 SHOLAPUR rd.
3. Density 40 vtm
4. Speed 30 (mi2h)
5. Location of Reg HQ TEMBHURNI.
6. Halts 20 mins every 2 hrs finishing at even numbered clock hr.
7. Staging area TEMBHURNI
8. Routes SHOLAPUR Rd.

Ser No	Fmn/Unit	Unit Distinguishing No	Number of vehs	TPP plus 50%	Routes to SP	Pass SP Head	Pass SP Tail	Remarks
(a)	(b)	(c)	(d)	(e)	(f)	(g)	(h)	(i)
	ARTY GP							
1	HQ Arty 1 Armd Div	40	11		..			
2	9 Para Fd Regt	72	148	24		0600	0624	Gp Comd to be detailed by HQ Arty.
3	One pl 649 Coy	84	30					
			189					
	ENGR GP							
4	HQ 623 Army Engr Gp	40	6					
5	40 Med Bty	71	22					Gp Comd to be detailed by HQ 623 Army Engr Gp
6	11 Fd Pk Coy	41	77	20	..	0635	0655	
7	7 Fd Coy	46	29					
8	Sec Pro Coy	43	4					
			138					

1. Date of Move 8 Aug 48.
2. SP Rd rail crossing 9852 SHOLAPUR rd.
3. Density 40 vtm
4. Speed 30 (m12h)
5. Location of Reg HQ TEMBHURN I.
6. Halts 20 mins every 2 hrs finishung at even numbered clock hr.
7. Staging area TEMBHURNI
8. Routes SHOLAPUR Rd.

Ser No	Fmn/Unit	Unit Distinguishing No	Number of vehs	TPP plus 50%	Route to SP	Pass SP		Remarks
						Head	Tail	
(a)	(b)	(c)	(d)	(e)	(f)	(g)	(h)	(i)
	REAR DIV HQ							
1	HQ Rear Div	40	37					
2	HQ 1 Armd Div Regt RIASC	40	8					
3	HQ CIAOC 1 Armd Div	40	1	12	..	0600	0612	Gp Comd to be detailed by HQ 1 Armd Div
4	HQ CIEME 1 Armd Div	40	3					
5	1 Armd Div OFP	40	34					
6	Sec and HQ Pro unit	43	18					
			101					
	MED GP							
7	ADMS 1 Armd Div	40	3	20	..	0620	0640	Gp Comd to be detailed by 649 GT Coy.
8	9 Lt Fd Amb	92	29					
9	6 Fd Surg Team	..	4					
10	649 Coy (less one pl) incl LAD & Comp Pl	84	82					
			118					

1. Date of Move 8 Aug 48.
2. SP Rd rail crossing 9852 SHOLAPUR rd.
3. Density 40 vtm
4. Speed 30 (mi2h)
5. Location of Reg HQ TEMBHURNI.
6. Halts 20 mins every 2 hrs finishing at even numbered clock hr.
7. Staging area TEMBHURNI
8. Routes SHOLAPUR Rd.

Ser No	Fmn/Unit	Unit Distinguishing No	Number of vehs	TPP plus 50%	Route to SP	Pass SP Head	Pass SP Tail	Remarks
(a)	(b)	(c)	(d)	(e)	(f)	(g)	(h)	(i)
	Wksp Gp							
11	128 Inf Wksp Coy	100	46					
12	1 Fd Regt (SP)	76	112	24	..	0650	0714	Gp Comd to be detailed by 1 Fd Regt.
13	103 Indep Rec Sec	102	6					
14	Det Svy Regt	..	9					
15	2 Indep Air OP Flt	..	12					
			186					

"EXERCISE SHIVAJI"

SECRET
No. 190 7-Q
Copy——
6 Aug 48

1 ARMD DIV MOVE ORDER No. 3.

1. **Gen**

   Ref 1 Armd Div Mov Order No 2 of 6 Aug 48 and HQ MC Group POONA rail Move Table.

2. **Composn Str**

   For train composn and str see appx A, B and C of MC Group POONA Rail Move Table.

3. **Rations**

   2 days fresh for journey and 3 days res to be carried.

4. **Water**

   Full water bottles will be carried. All water drawn en route will be chlorinated.

5. **Loading and unloading**

   Rolling stock will be available for loading at KIRKEE Siding by 0900 hrs and will be completed by 1400 hrs the same day. Units will ensure that trains are unloaded without delay, on arrival at SHOLAPUR.

6. **Escorts**

   Min of 2 men per flat will be detailed one of whom should be a trained driver.

7. **Discipline**

   Attention of OC trains is drawn to the following orders for strict compliance.
   IAO 18/S/44 Discipline of troops travelling by rail.
   IAO 65/45 Encouragement of beggars.
   IAO 28/S/44 Anti-malaria precautions.
   IAO 1887/43 Escorts for MT vehs by rail.

8. **OC Train**

OC train will be detailed from units as mentioned below:

Appx 'A' Serial A 1 Fd Regt
        Serial B 34(M) A/Tk Regt
        Serial C 1 Fd Regt
        Serial D 1 Fd Regt
        Serial E 1 Fd Regt

                        Sd/- HAR PARSAD
                                    Lt Col
                              AA and QMG

Method——SDS
Time of Signature——1600
Time issued to Sigs——1630

Distribution

    1 Armd Bde
    3 IND GRS
    Arty
    Engrs
    Sigs
    ST
    Med
    Ord
    EME
    Pro
    HQ Sqn
    GS
    A
    South Comd
    POONA Sub Area
    SHOLAPUR (I) Sub Area
    7 Inf Bde
    9 Inf Bde
    SSD POONA
    RTO POONA
    RTO SHOLAPUR
    MC Gp POONA

Appx E to 1 ARMD DIV in Op "POLO"

SECRET

Copy——

30 Aug 48

CR/1741/8/GS

1 ARMD DIV OO No 3

Ref maps 1 in to 4 miles—sheets 47 N, 47 O, 56 B, 56 C and 56 G.

INFM

1. **Enemy**

    (a) Units and locations of the Hyderabad Army are given at Appx "A."

    (b) Since the issue of OO No 2 of 16 Jul 48, more arms may have been flown into HYDERABAD and it is reliably reported that they have 24 dual purpose BOFORS guns and that muzzle loaders are being converted into A-tank role. MT, though in a bad condition, had been improved by the requisitioning of spare parts from the civ markets.

    (c) HYDERABAD State is rapidly forming its RAZAKARS and refugees, many of whom are ex-soldiers of the IA, into formed bns, to assist their army.

    (d) The enemy is aware that our main thrust will be along the SHOLAPUR-NALDRUG-TALMUD-ZAHIRABAD-HYDERABAD rd. His plans however appear to be mainly def and he hopes to hold our adv by demolitions and by holding posns at NALDRUG-UMARGA-TALMUD-ZAHIRABAD and SADASEOPET. His tps stationed to the NORTH and SOUTH of this rd will try to reinf their own forces and also to harass our L of C. The irregulars and PATHANS will undoubtedly try to do the latter rather than meet us in a pitched battle.

    (e) The morale of the regular state forces cannot be called high, though they will undoubtedly fight hard to save themselves from extermination. The morale of the irregulars is high and will remain so until they take a good knock.

2. **Own Tps**

(a) See OO No 2 of 16 Jul 48.

(b) 9 Inf Bde Gp as a subsidiary to the ops detailed here are capturing TULJAPUR, establishing the MEWAR Inf there, clearing from the SOUTH the rd SHOLAPUR-TULJAPUR and then advancing along the rd TULJAPUR-LOHARA-YENAGUR.

(c) After 1 MEWAR Inf have occupied TULJAPUR they are to move a part of their unit NORTH to OSMANABAD to capture it. For any ops of 1 MEWAR Inf after TULJAPUR, they will revert to comd of SHOLAPUR (I) Sub Area.

(d) WILCOL, which will be reinforced by 3/11 GR less one coy at BARSI, will be doing an op to show force in the direction of OSMANABAD and to capture YERMALA. On D day this force, though doing a task assigned by us, will revert to comd of POONA Sub-Area, who can then use them on other tasks later.

(e) On D day, RIAF ac in sp of this op are carrying out the following tasks :—

   (i) Tac R on the rds
   NALDRUG-HYDERABAD up to ZAHIRABAD
   HOMNABAD-BIDAR-ZAHIRABAD
   YENAGUR-ALAND-GULBARGA-HOMNABAD

   with the object of reporting all mov NORTH and WEST.

   (ii) RIAF ac are attacking all MT moving on these rds in a WESTERLY and NORTHERLY direction, mil conc in the villages of MORAM and ALAND and opportunity targets as seen or as directed by the VCP.

   (iii) *BOMB LINES* on D day are :—
   Up to 1000 hrs
   rd—Nullah X QA 6703—along rd to YENAGUR—thence along rd to ALAND excl MORAM QF 9157 and ALAND.

After 1000 hrs

rd—Nullah X QA 6703—rd—Nullah X QG 0488—along rd to UMARGA QG 0963—thence along rd to ALAND.

INTENTION

3. 1 Armd Div will capture NALDRUG and exploit as far as UMARGA.

METHOD

4. The op will be carried out in three phases:—

Phase 1—By 7 Inf Bde Gp

(a) Capture of NALDRUG br intact from the SOUTH.
(b) The occupation of JALKOT and the capture or destruction of any guns in or near that village.
(c) The prevention of mil mov by the HYDERABAD forces on the rd NALDRUG-HYDERABAD.

Phase 2—By 1 Armd Bde Gp

(a) The capture of NALDRUG town from the WEST
(b) The est of 4 GWALIOR Inf in NALDRUG.
(c) Exploitation EAST of NALDRUG to YENAGUR if possible.

Phase 3—By STRIKE FORCE

Exploitation to UMARGA and the est of a firm base there.

Phase 1

5. **Tps**

HQ 7 Inf Bde

with under comd—

One bty 34(M) A Tk Regt
Det 65 Fd Coy
2 R SIKH
3 IND GRS
Det 85 Fd Amb
Det 1 Armd Bde Sec Coy
Det 128 Inf Wksp Coy
One sec 1 Armd Div Pro

6. **Objectives**

   (a) Capture of NALDRUG br by 0400 hrs D day.
   (b) Occupation of JALKOT by 0400 hrs D day.
   (c) Capture or destruction of enemy guns in JALKOT area.
   (d) Prevention of mil mov on rd NALDRUG-HYDERABAD.

   The State border will NOT be crossed till 2000 hrs D minus 1 day.

7. **Axis of Adv**

   KAJIKANBAS QF 6949—LOHGAON QF 7255—NALDRUG br.

8. **Success Sig**

   By wrls—Codeword **BUNDI** for capture of NALDRUG br
   Codeword **KOTHA** for capture of JALKOT
   Codeword **BHOPAL** for capture of guns.

   Phase 2

9. **Tps**

   HQ 1 Armd Bde
      with under comd—
         3 CAV less two sqns
         17 HORSE less one sqn
         1 Fd Regt less one bty
         Det 7 Fd Coy
         One coy 9 DOGRA
         14 RAJPUT
         4 GWALIOR Inf
         One coy 85 Fd Amb
         Det 1 Armd Bde Rec Coy
         Det 5 Armd Wksp Coy
         One sec 1 Armd Div Pro Unit
         One VCP

10. **Objectives**

    (a) NALDRUG town.
    (b) The blocking with 4 GWALIOR Inf of rds into NALDRUG from NORTH and SOUTH.

(c) Sp of 7 Inf Bde Gp if in difficulties.
(d) Exploitation to YENAGUR if possible.

11. **Axis of adv**

    rd SHOLAPUR-NALDRUG

12. **Report Lines**

    ITKAL QF 5456 codeword **JUMNA**
    KERUR QF 5658 codeword **GANGA**

13. **Timings**

    No mov from conc area till 0400 hrs D day. Leading tps at NALDRUG br as soon after as possible and NOT later than 0630 hrs D day

14. **Success Sig**

    By wrls—codeword **ALWAR** for capture of NALDRUG.

Phase 3

15. **Tps**

    STRIKE FORCE

    Comd : Lt Col RAM SINGH
    Tps : 1 HORSE less one sqn
    One bty 1 Fd Regt
    2 Bty 40 Med Regt
    Det Engrs
    9 DOGRA less one coy
    One Coy 9 Lt Fd Amb
    One VCP

16. **Objectives**

    (a) Exploitation to UMARGA.
    (b) Blocking of the rds running NORTH and SOUTH from UMARGA.
    (c) The est of a firm base at UMARGA.

17. **Axis of adv**

    rd SHOLAPUR-HYDERABAD.

18. **Bounds**

    X rds QF 8765—codeword **BEAS**
    Nullah rd X QG 0265—codeword **SUTLEJ**

19. **Time**

On orders from this HQ. NOT before 0700 hrs D day.

Gen

20. **Concs**

The orders for conc of the forces for the above op are given in Appx "B" to this order. Tps NOT specifically mentioned in this order or Appx "B," will remain in their present locations till called fwd.

21. **Axis of adv**

Div axis of adv will be rd SHOLAPUR-HYDERABAD

ADM

22. Adm orders for this op issue separately.

INTERCOMN

23. Wrls comn will be provided as in Appx "C." Detailed instrs will be issued by Sigs.

24. Immediate air sp will be demanded over the A1 net, otherwise on the A2 net.

25. The movs of Tac and Main Div HQ will be notified as and when they occur.

(Sd.) UMRAO SINGH
Lt Col
GSO 1

ACK

Time of signature................hrs.
Time issued to sigs............hrs.
Method of issue................
Distribution—see separate sheet att.

DISTRIBUTION LIST

Ref to 1 Armd Div OO No 3 of 30 Aug 48

	Copy No.
1 Armd Bde	1-3
7 Inf Bde	4-6
9 Inf Bde	7-9
9 DOGRA	10-11
Arty	12-13
Engrs	14
Sigs	15-16
SHOLAPUR (I) Sub Area	17
South Comd	18-27
Comd	28
G	29-31
I	32
AQ	33-35
ST	36
Med	37
Ord	38
EME	39
Pro	40
RIAF	41
RIAF Liaison Officer	42
File	43-44
WAR Diary	45-47
Spare	48-55

SECRET
Appx 'A'
Ref 1 Armd Div OO
No 3 of Aug 48
Copy No.————

xxvi

ORDER OF BATTLE
HYDERABAD STATE FORCES

Refers to 1 Armd Div OO No. 3 of 30 Aug 48.

Ref map HYDERABAD 1/1,000,000

The State is divided into zonal sectors as follows:—

Sri No	SECTORS	HQ	AREA COVERED	Map Ref	UNITS	NAMES OF COMD
1.	NORTHERN SECTOR	AURANGABAD	Dist AURANGABAD do PARBHANI do NANDED do ADILABAD do NIZAMABAD	7519 7619 7719 7819 7818	8 HI, 7 HI	BRIG TAUFIQ ALI
2.	EASTERN SECTOR	KHAMMAMET	Dist NALGONDA do WARANGAL do KARIMNAGAR	7917 7917 7918	1 HI, 4 HI, 1 NI, 1 GT COY 1 Comp Pl M LAD	BRIG MOHD HASSAN KHAN
3.	SOUTHERN SECTOR	YADGIR	Dist GULBARGA do RAICHUR do MAHBOOBNAGAR	7617 7716 7716	9 HR, 10 HR 11 HR	LT COL ALI AHMED
4.	WESTERN SECTOR	BIDAR	Dist BIDAR do OSMANABAD do BIR	7717 7618 7518	3 GI, 1 HI 2 HI, 3 HI 2 GT, COY, 2 COMP PL, "A" FD BTY	BRIG SYEEDY HABIB AHMED
5.	HYDERABAD AREA	HYDERABAD	Dist MEDAK do ATRAF-I-BALDA	7818 7817	2 HI, 4 GI, 5 HI, 6HI, 12 HI, (13 & 14 HI BEING RAISED) JAMIAT NIZAM MAHBOOBIA N G B FOUR IRREGULAR BDES	

No	FMNS	UNITS	SUB UNITS	Locations		NAMES OF COMD	REMARKS
				NAMES OF PLACES	MAP REF		
(a)	(b)	(c)	(d)	(e)	(f)	(g)	(h)
1.	HQ HA			HYDERABAD	7817	ARMY COMD-MAJ GEN S A EL-EDROOS DEPUTY COMD—BRIG ASHRAF AHMED BGS—COL H D H Y NAPEAN DSO COL IC ADM —COL HANIF RAHAT GSO 1—LT COL AFSAR ALI BEG AAG—LT COL M M ZAKI AQ—LT COL SAFDAR HUSSAM GOHAR SIGS—LT COL NABI KHAN, GSO 1 ST—LT COL M M ALI, GSO 1	
2.	OFFRS SCHOO			HYDERABAD	7817		
3.	HATC	BASIC TRG INF WING MECH WING ARTY WING HORSED CAV WING		HYDERABAD	7817	LT COL WESTON	ASAFNAGAR LINES
4.	HAOD			GOLCONDA	7817		

				Locations			
No	FMNS	UNITS	SUB UNITS	NAMES OF PLACES	MAP REF	NAMES OF COMD	REMARKS
(a)	(b)	(c)	(d)	(e)	(f)	(g)	(h)
5.	HASC	HYDERABAD SUP COY	1 COMP PL 2 COMP PL 3 COMP PL	HYDERABAD LATUR KHAMMAMET	7817 7618 8017	CAPT WARRIS HASSAN KHAN	Sup pt at MAMNOOR do OSMANABAD do BIDAR do JALNA do YADGIR
		1 GT COY		BIDAR	7717		
		2 GT COY		KHAMMAMET	8017		
		3 GT COY		HYDERABAD	7817		
6.	HFER			HYDERABAD	7817		HYDERABAD ENGR REGT
7.	HEME	COMD WKSP		HYDERABAD	7817	MAJ CRAGIE	
		2ND LINE WKSP		HYDERABAD			
		1 FD PK COY		HYDERABAD			
		1 FD SQN		HYDERABAD			With printing sec
		1 PNR COY		HYDERABAD			
		1 LAD		KHAMMAMET	8017	Lt ABDUL MAJEED	
		2 LAD		BIDAR	7717	Lt BALARAM	
		3 LAD		HYDERABAD	7817		
8.	HYDERABAD SIG REGT	1 WRLS SEC		BIDAR	7717		With an extensive wrls net connecting all fwd units.

9.		2 WRLS SEC		YADGIR	7716	
	HAMC	3 WRLS SEC		KHAMMAMET	8017	
		FD AMB		HYDERABAD		
10.	PRO DET	VET CORPS		HYDERABAD		
11.	SECURITY SECTION			HYDERABAD		
12.	HYDERABAD FD REGT			HYDERABAD		
		"A" BTY		NALDRUG	7617	5 × 25 PR GUNS (2 AT NALDRUG AND 2 AT JALKOT)
		"B" BTY		?		5 × 25 PR GUNS
		"C" BTY		HYDERABAD	7817	6 × 18 PR GUNS
13.	HCB			HYDERABAD	7817	(HYDERABAD CAV BDE)
		1 HL	LESS TWO SQNS	SURIAPET	7917	LT COL MOHD ARIFUD-DIN — Mechanised
			TWO SQNS	KODAR	7916	
		2 HL		SECUNDERABAD	7817	LT COL YUSUF ALI BEG — Mechanised
		3 GL	LESS TWO SQNS	YERMALA	7518	LT COL ASADULLAH KHAN — Partly mechanised partly horsed
			ONE SQN	BIR	7518	
			ONE SQN	OSMANABAD	7618	
		4 HL	LESS TWO SQNS	BONAKALU	8017	LT COL ZAKI BILGRAMI — Tp at TULJAPUR
			ONE SQN	MADHRA	8016	
			ONE SQN	CHINTAKANI	8017	Mechanised

No	FMNS	UNITS	SUB UNITS	Locations		NAMES OF COMD	REMARKS
				NAMES OF PLACES	MAP REF		
(a)	(b)	(c)	(d)	(e)	(f)	(g)	(h)
14.	1 HIB			BIDAR	7717	Brig G. M. T. CHAMA-RETTE	B M BILAL AHMED JEDDY
		1 HI	Less three coys	TALMUD	7617	LT COL MIRZA HIMAYAT BEG	
			Tac HQ plus two coys	NALDRUG	7617		
			One coy	NALDRUG TALMUD	7617		
		2 HI	Less two coys	LATUR	7618	LT COL YAHAYA ABIDI	
			One coy	MURUDA KAOL	7618		
			One coy	DHOKI	7616		
		3 HI		BIDAR	7717		
15.	2 HIB	5 HI	Less two coys	HYDERABAD	7817	LT COL WAHEED	Coys deployed in area BIDAR-ZAHIRABAD
		6 HI		HYDERABAD	7817		
		7 HI		HYDERABAD	7817	LT COL USHAQ AHMED	
			One coy	NANDER	7719		
			One coy	HINGOLI	7719		

16.	8 HI	..	Less two coys	AURANGABAD JALNA	7519 7519	LT COL MUNIR SIDDIQUE
			"B" Coy	KANNAD	7540	
	HRB	..	"C" Coy	RAICHUR	7716	
	9 HR	..	HQ	YADGIR	7716	LT COL ZAFAR ALI KHAN
			Two coys	SHORAPUR	7616	
			Two coys	SHAHPUR	7616	
	10 HR	..	Less three coys	RAICHUR	7716	LT COL SHAFAR ULLA QURESHI, SC
			One coy	MUDGAL	7716	Guarding br over rivers KISTNA and TUNGA-BHADRA
			One coy	GANGAWATI MANVI	7615 7715	
			One coy	KUSHTAGI	7615	
	11 HR	..	Less one coy	GULBARGA	7617	LT COL MOHD KAMAL-UDDIN AHMED
			One coy	SHAHABAD	7617	
17.	3 HIB	..		HYDERABAD	7817	Just raised
	12 HI	..		HYDERABAD	7817	
	13 HI	..		HYDERABAD	7817	
	14 HI	..		HYDERABAD	7817	Being raised
18.	NAZAM BDE	..		HYDERABAD	7817	
	NIZAM'S BODY GUARD		Less two sqns	HYDERABAD	7817	
			One sqn	KHAMMAMET	8017	
			One sqn	MANCHERIAL	7918	

No	FMNS	UNITS	SUB UNITS	Locations – NAMES OF PLACES	Locations – MAP REF	NAMES OF COMD	REMARKS
(a)	(b)	(c)	(d)	(e)	(f)	(g)	(h)
		1 NI	Less two coys	MAMNOOR (WARANGAL)	7917	LT COL HABIB AHMED	
			ADV HQ 1	KATAGUDEM	8017		
			One coy	ASHRAOPET WIRA	8117		
		2 NI	Less one coy	HYDERABAD			
		3 NI	One coy	NANDED	7719		
19.	HY'BAD HOUSE HOLD BDE	4 GI		HYDERABAD		BRIG HABIB HASNUDDIN	Being withdrawn
		JAMAYAT NIZAM MAHBOOBIA GRN BN		HYDERABAD			Being raised
20.	SARF-I-KHAS BDE (IRREGULAR)	1st SARF-I-KHAS INF		HYDERABAD		BRIG SHEKH BASHIR	Being issued with modern weapons and converted into regular units
		2nd do		HYDERABAD			
		3rd do					25% Modern arms rest Henry Martins

21	PAIGAH BDE (IRREGULAR)				Poorly armed with out-of-date weapons
	JANUMALLAH LANCERS do INF		HYDERABAD		
	ASMANJA INF		HYDERABAD		
	LUTFUD-DOWALLAH CAV 1 SQN		HYDERABAD		
22.	ARAB BDE (IRREGULAR)		HYDERABAD	Lt Col RIASAT ALI MIRZA	
	1st ARAB BN	..	HYDERABAD		Armed with muzzle loaders
	2nd do	..	HYDERABAD		
	3rd do	..	HYDERABAD		
23.	REFUGEE BDE (IRREGULAR)			MAJ SYED TAJMUL HUSSAIN	
	1st BN	Less three coys	GULBARGA	7617	Two more refugee bde being raised. Target date 30 Oct
		One coy ..	ALAND	7617	
		One coy ..	KULALI	7617	
		One coy ..	HUNSGI	7616	
	2nd BN	..	WARANGAL QF	7917	Deployed along the border to assist det 1 ni add 4 hi
	3rd BN	..	NALGONDA QF	7917	Str only 550
	4th BN	..	NIZAMABAD QF	7818	Str only two coys

No	FMNS	UNITS	SUB UNITS	LOCATIONS		NAMES OF COMD	REMARKS
				NAMES OF PLACES	MAP REF		
(a)	(b)	(c)	(d)	(e)	(f)	(g)	(h)
24.	RAZAKARS BNS	Two bns		AURANGABAD DIST	7519		
		Two bns		PARBHANI-DIST	7619		
		Two bns		NANDED-HINGOLI	7719	More bns are being raised
		One bn		ADILABAD	7819		
		One bn		NIZAMABAD	7818		
		Two bns		HYDERABAD	7817		
25.	PATHAN BNS			GULBARGA	7617		Small dets deployed along border from Aland to Kushtagi. Two more bns will be raised as soon as manpower is available. Target date 30 Oct

SECRET
Appx " B "
Ref 1 Armd Div OO
No 3 of 30 Aug 48
Copy No.———

CONC MOVS BEFORE D DAY

Refers to 1 Armd Div OO No 30 Aug 48

1. To enable units to get to their op posns before D day the following conc moves will take place as given below.

2. These moves will not be worked on a D day basis as D may be delayed owing to weather or other factors. The codeword for conc moves will be **OVER POWER** and on receiving this codeword, comds will order the following moves, starting on the day subsequent to receipt of the codeword. The day conc moves commence will be known as **W day**

3. **1 Armd Bde** (rd SHOLAPUR-NALDRUG)

   (a) **W and W plus 1 day**

   (i) All units of the bde gp taking part in the first day ops, to an area NORTH of the rd SHOLAPUR-NALDRUG and between ms 163.2 and TANDULWADI. The majority of the units will be kept behind the high ground WEST of TANDULWADI. The rd will NOT be used by any vehs except those ordered by 1 Armd Bde for these two days and timings will be issued direct to units moving by 1 Armd Bde. The only exception to this will be sigs DR vehs. Pro arrangements for ensuring correct move will be arranged by 1 Armd Div.

   (ii) All moves will incl " B " echs.

   (iii) 1 Armd Bde will infm Main Div HQ of any units of its gp which will be required for ops later but will NOT be moving on the original conc, by 1000 hrs W plus 1. One comd will be nominated for all such units, who will be in wrls touch with 1 Armd Bde and whose name will be intimated to Main Div HQ. This does NOT incl " D " ech units.

(b) **W plus 2 day**

The rd SHOLAPUR-NALDRUG will be allotted to 1 Armd Bde up to 0700 hrs after which it must be clear. From 1600 hrs to 1900 hrs, the rd will be allotted once again to 1 Armd Bde for main vehs.

4. **7 Inf Bde** (rd SHOLAPUR-AKALKOT-WAGDARI)

   (a) **W and W plus 1 day**

   7 Inf Bde gp as shown in this OO to AKALKOT with one bn to WAGDARI. Units will move direct on to the AKALKOT rd from their present camp sites without coming into SHOLAPUR, to avoid clashing with 1 Armd Bde. A cross country route will be recced forthwith.

   (b) **W plus 2 day**

   (i) Tac HQ 7 Bde, 2 R SIKH, 3 IND GRS — by march route to KAJI-KANBAS. The main number of vehs, as discussed between GOC and Comd 7 Inf Bde may accompany.

   (ii) This move on W plus 2 day will only take place however, on 7 Bde receiving from Main Div HQ the codeword **SATURATION**.

   (c) For purposes of security, only two recces will be allowed fwd from AKALKOT and WAGDARI to KAJI-KANBAS. The strength of these recce parties will NOT exceed ten all ranks and two vehs.

   (d) All orders and timings for the above movs and orders for pro arrangements will be issued by 7 Inf Bde.

5. **9 Inf Bde** (rd SHOLAPUR-BARSI)

   (a) **W plus 1 day**

   One sqn 3 CAV, One bty 9 Para Fd Regt RIA, 2/1 GR. — by MT to BARSI via NANAJ.

   (b) **W plus 2 day**

   The above force to an RV near the TULJAPUR border as arranged by Comd 9 Inf Bde. This mov on W plus 2 day will only take place however, on 9 Inf Bde receiving from Main Div HQ the codeword **SATURATION**.

   (c) All orders and timings for movs and Pro arrangements will be issued by 9 Inf Bde.

6. **Moves of Misc Units**

   (a) *Main Div HQ* .. Will move on W plus 2 to an area just behind 1 Armd Bde Gp; the site to be selected by 1 Armd Bde. Size of area required 600 yds by 300 yds and adjoining the rd. Recce parties will leave camp 0945 hrs and mov will be completed by 1230 hrs.

   (b) *Engr gp with bridging eqpt* .. Will move on W plus 2 day to area ms 162.4 rd SHOLAPUR-NALDRUG. Recce parties will leave at 1200 hrs; mov will be completed by 1430 hrs.

   (c) *Two coys MEWAR Inf* .. Will move on W plus 2 day from NANAJ back to their base at SHOLAPUR. They will be relieved by one coy KOLHAPUR RAJARAM Rifles under arrangements of SHOLAPUR (I)SubArea. Mov to be completed by 1200 hrs.

   (d) *One MDS* .. To move to vicinity TANDULWADI on rd SHOLAPUR-NALDRUG on W plus 2 day Recce parties will report to 1 Armd Bde for site at 0730 hrs on W plus 2 and main party will be clear of ms 163 by 1000 hrs.

7. **ADM**

   During the period of conc, maint will be as it is now. The adm arrangements as given in this OO will only come into being from D day. The only exceptions to this will be

   (a) 6 × 3-ton vehs of sec line will replenish the force at BARSI on the evening of W plus 1 with POL and return to SHOLAPUR the same day.

   (b) 2 × 3-ton vehs of sec line will replenish 7 Bde at AKALKOT on evening of W plus 1 with POL and return same day.

Lt Col
GSO 1

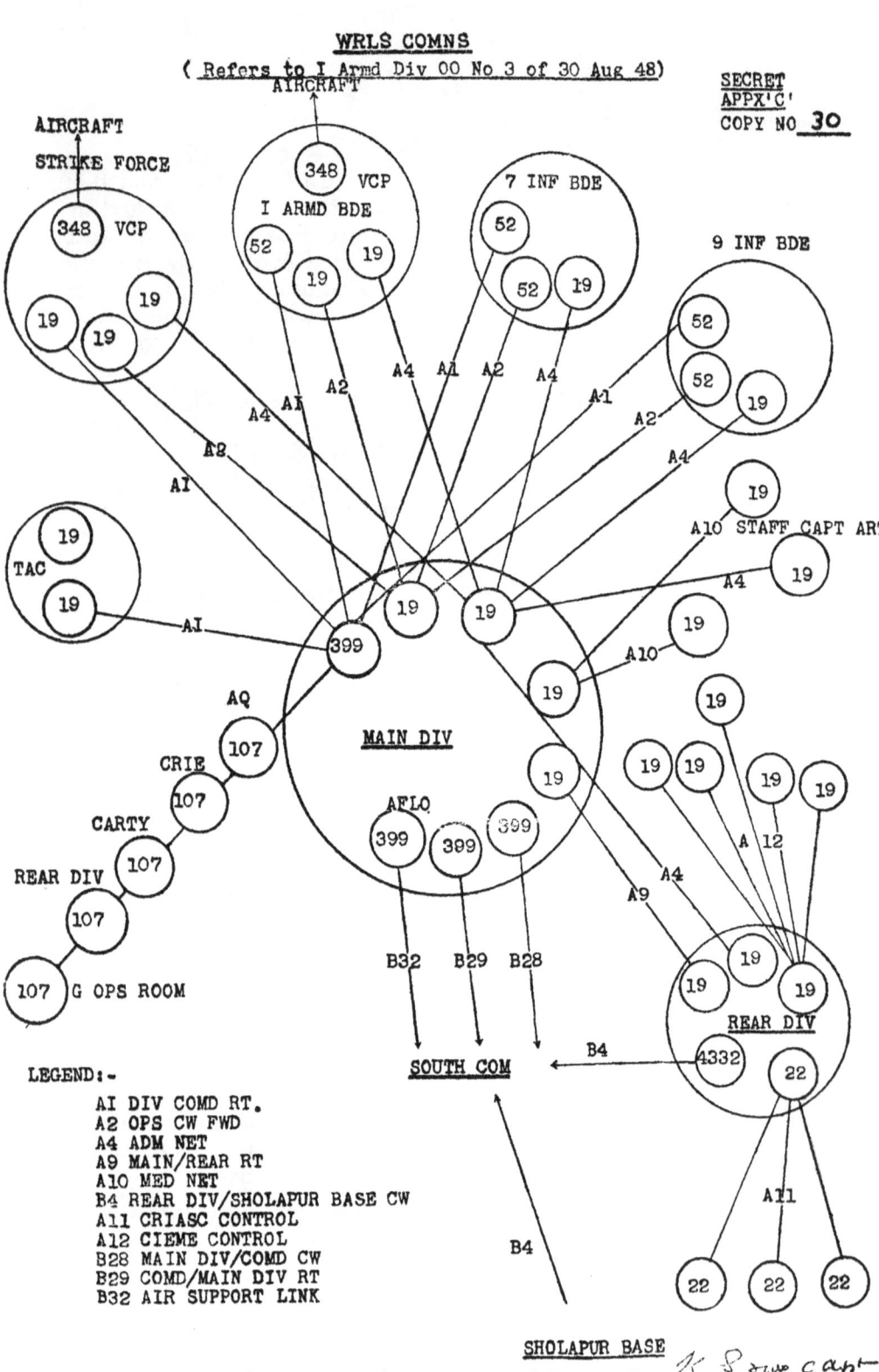

3/2 PUNJAB
1 BIHAR
2/1 GR
One coy 84 Fd Amb
Det 120 Wksp Coy
Det 5 Inf Div Pro Coy
    plus
1 MEWAR Inf till the occupation of TULJAPUR.

4. **TASKS IN GEN**

Your task in gen will be the capture of TULJAPUR, the est of MEWAR Inf there and a subsequent adv to LOHARA and on to YENAGUR where you will est contact with tps as detailed in OO No. 3 of 30 Aug 48, moving along the rd NALDRUG-UMARGA.

5. **TASKS IN PARTICULAR**

   (a) The capture of TULJAPUR, in order to achieve surprise, will be done from the direction of BARSI by one bn, one sqn 3 CAV and one bty 9 Para Fd Regt. The attack on TULJAPUR will go in at first lt on the morning of D day.

   (b) The remainder of your force will move as discussed by us along the rd SHOLAPUR-TULJAPUR and this rd will be reserved solely for your use on D day.

   (c) On capturing TULJAPUR, you will est MEWAR Inf there as soon as possible and give them orders to block the rds SHOLAPUR-TULJAPUR, TULJAPUR-NALDRUG and to exploit NORTHWARDS with the object of securing OSMANABAD. For this purpose should you so consider necessary you will leave one bty 9 Para Fd Regt in sp of them. You will NOT leave the tp of 18 Cav at TULJAPUR. Once you have directed MEWAR Inf on to their task they will revert for comd to SHOLAPUR (I) Sub Area. The time you hand them over will be notified to me and to SHOLAPUR (I) Sub Area. The latter can be done through MEWAR Inf who should have a wrls link back to SHOLAPUR (I) Sub Area.

   (d) You will NOT adv beyond YENAGUR till further orders. You will try to reach YENAGUR by 1800 hrs D day.

ADM

6. You will be full up in your echs before you move off and the tps conc at BARSI will carry the extra replenishment of sups and POL required in their own tpt, except for six 3-ton POL sec line vehs which will replenish tks in BARSI on W plus 1. NO sec line tpt will move to replenish you along the route you have taken and your first replenishment will be on D plus 1, at a pt on the rd SHOLAPUR-HYDERABAD.

7. You will open an ADS at TULJAPUR as soon as you can. This will be cleared by the ADMS from the amb Cs at his disposal direct to the CCS SHOLAPUR. When all mil cas as a result of the TULJAPUR op have been cleared, the ADS will close and join you in your further adv. Cas incurred later by 1 MEWAR Inf, will be held by them in a RAP est at TULJAPUR and will be cleared under arrangements of SHOLAPUR (I) Sub Area.

INTERCOMN

8. You will be linked to 1 Armd Div by wrls as shown in Appx "C" to OO No. 3 of 30 Aug 48.

9. You will report by wrls your mov as follows:—

    (a) Capture of TULJAPUR—Codeword **JAIPUR**

    (b) Head reaches LOHARA—Codeword **JODHPUR**

    (c) Head reaches YENAGUR—Codeword **JAISALMER**.

ACK   J. N. CHAUDHURI

Time of signature................hrs.   Maj Gen

Time issued to sigs..............hrs   Comd

Method of issue......................

Distribution—List att

DISTRIBUTION LIST

Refers to Op Instr No 1 of 30 Aug 48

	Copy No
Brig S. D. VERMA, Comd 1 Armd Bde ..	2
Brig GURBACHAN SINGH, Comd 7 Inf. Bde.	3
Lt Col RAM SINGH, Comd 'STRIKE FORCE'	4
Lt Col DALIP SINHA, Comd MEWAR Inf .	5
Brig S. N. BHATIA, Comd SHOLAPUR (I) Sub Area	6
South Comd	8
G	9-10
A/Q	11-12
RIAF	13
File	14-15
War Diary	16-19

MAP Q

DISPOSITIONS OF TROOPS AS AT 1800 HRS ON D MINUS 1 AND D DAYS
MAP Q 1 ARMOURED DIVISION IN OPERATION POLO

(Note.—Arrows indicate projected moves)

SCALE 1 INCH TO 8 MILES

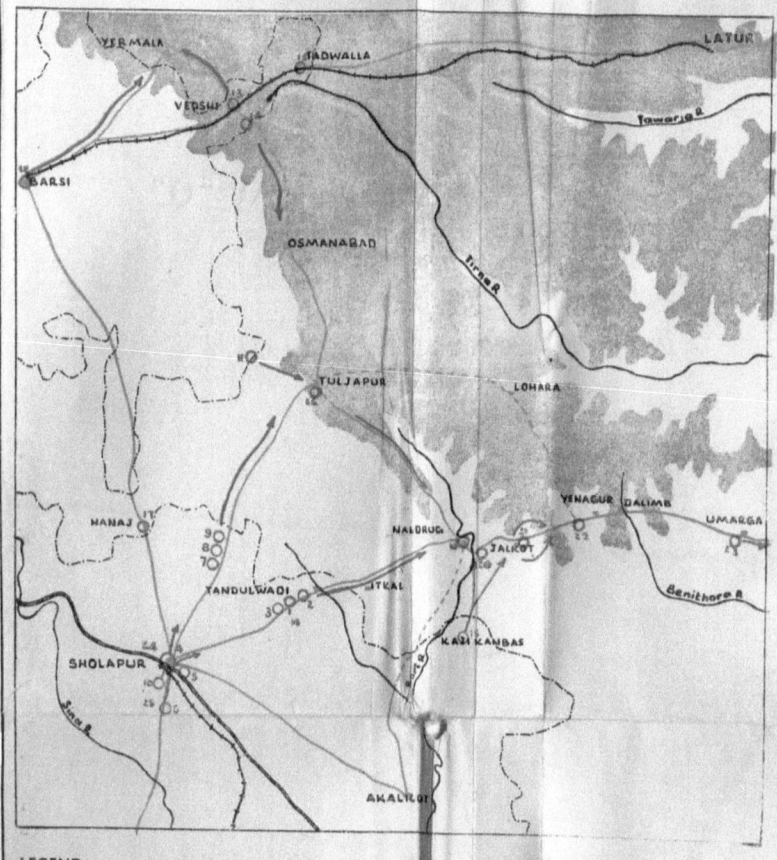

LEGEND

D MINUS 1 DAY (RED)

1. Main HQ 1 Armd Div
2. HQ 1 Armd Bde
   17 HORSE less one sqn
   3 CAV less two sqn
   1 Fd Regt RIA
   14 RAJPUT
   One coy 9 DOGRA
3. Engrs
4. HQ SHOLAPUR (1) sub Area
5. Strike Force
   1 HORSE less one sqn
   9 DOGRA less one coy
   2 Bty 40 Med Regt RIA
6. Rear HQ 1 Armd Div
   One sqn 1 HORSE
   26 LAA Regt RIA less two btys
7. HQ 9 Inf Bde
   One coy 1 BIHAR
   9 Para Fd Regt RIA less two btys
8. MEWAR Inf
9. Tp 18 CAV
   3/2 PUNJAB
   One bty 9 Para Fd Regt RIA
10. 1 BIHAR less one coy
11. One sqn 3 CAV
    2/1 GR
    One bty 9 Para Fd Regt RIA
12. Sqn 8 CAV
    One coy 3/11 GR
13. One tp 8 CAV
    One coy less one pl 3/11 GR
14. 8 CAV less two sqns and one tp
15. One pl 3/11 GR
16. HQ 7 Inf Bde
    One bty 34 (M) ATK Regt (SP)
    2 R SIKH
    3 IND GRS
17. RAJA RAM Rif

D DAY (GREEN)

18. Main HQ 1 Armd Div
19. 4 GWALIOR Inf
20. 3 IND GRS
21. HQ 7 Inf Bde
    One bty 34 (M) ATK Regt RIA
    2 R SIKH
22. HQ 1 Armd Bde
    3 CAV less two sqns
    17 HORSE less one sqn
    1 Fd Regt RIA less one bty
    One coy 9 DOGRA
    14 RAJPUT
23. Strike Force
    1 HORSE less one sqn
    9 DOGRA less one coy
    2 Bty 40 Med Regt RIA
    One bty 1 Fd Regt (SP)
24. HQ SHOLAPUR (1) Sub Area
25. Rear HQ 1 Armd Div
    One Sqn 1 HORSE
    26 LAA Regt RIA less two btys
26. HQ 9 Inf Bde
    3/2 PUNJAB
    2/1 GR
    1 BIHAR
    One sqn 3 Cav
    9 Para Fd Regt RIA

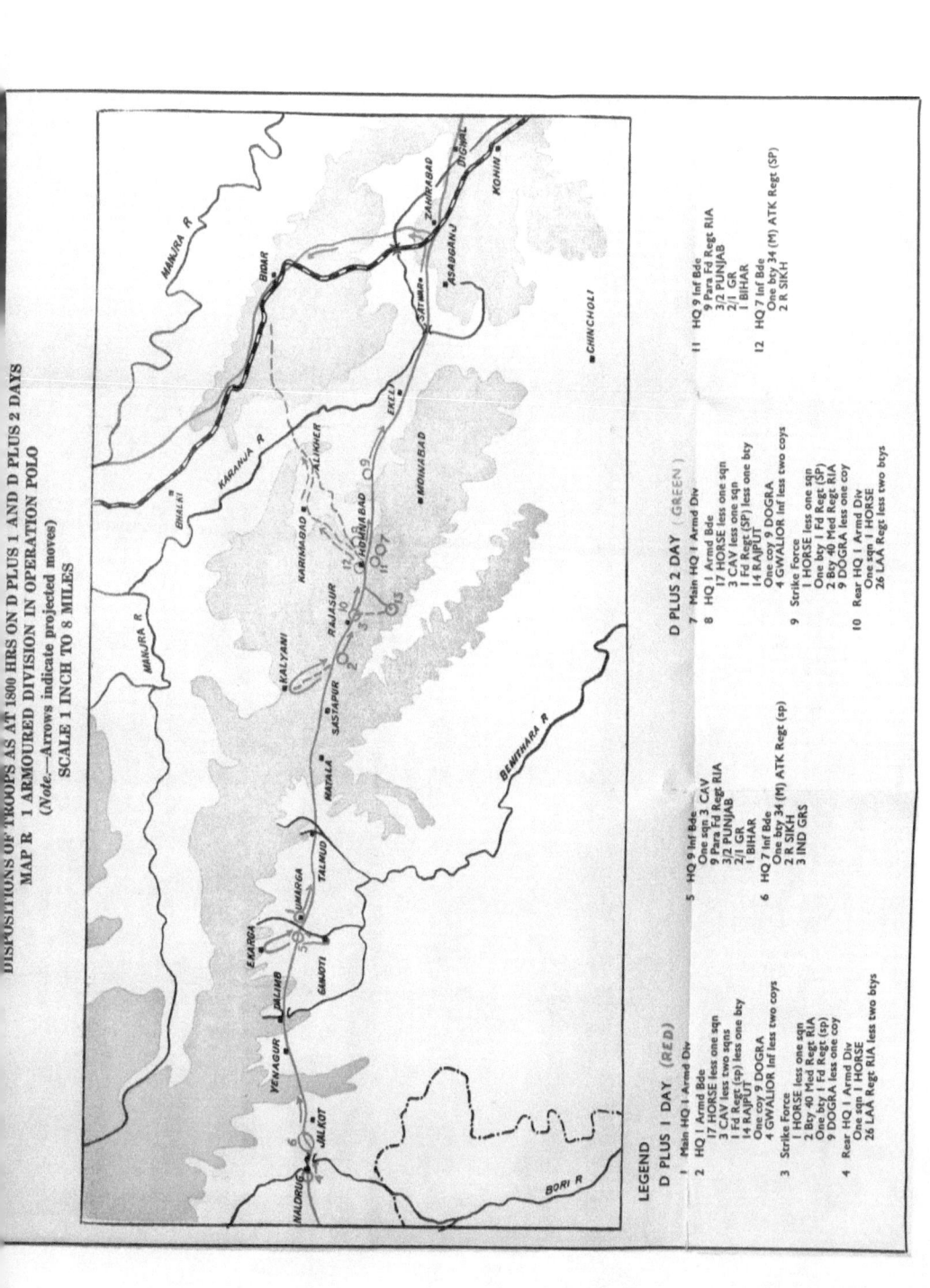

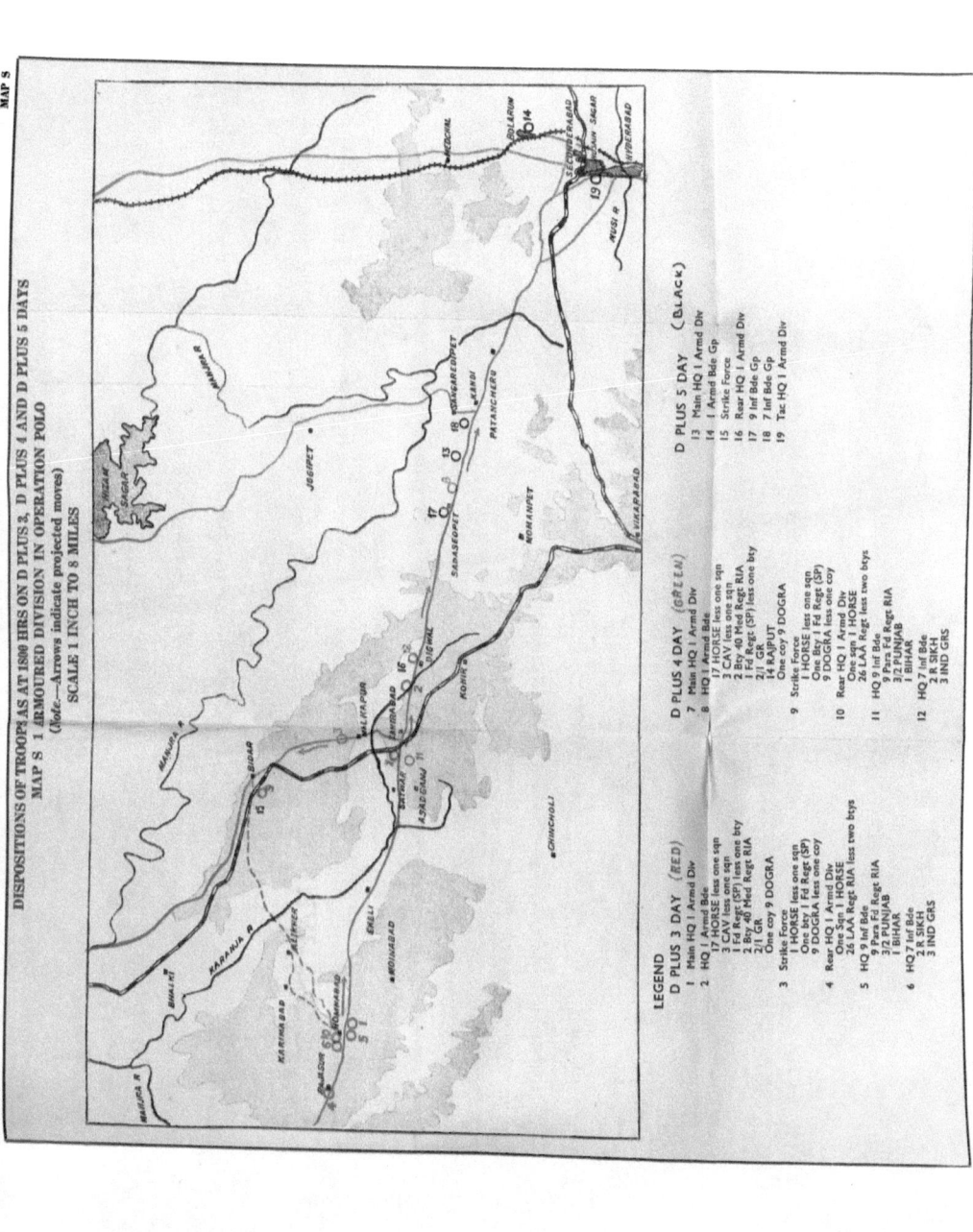

www.ingramcontent.com/pod-product-compliance
Lightning Source LLC
Chambersburg PA
CBHW021357300426
44114CB00012B/1272